SPOTLESS
PETS

Titles by
Shannon Lush and Jennifer Fleming

Spotless	*Save*
Spotless 2	*Completely Spotless*
Speedcleaning	*Spotless A–Z*
How to be Comfy	*Spotless Baby*

Title by
Shannon and Erin Lush
Kids Can Clean

Title by
Shannon Lush and Trent Hayes
Stainless

Title by
Jennifer Fleming and Anna-Louise Bouvier
The Feel Good Body

Title by
Adam Ferrier and Jennifer Fleming
The Advertising Effect

SPOTLESS PETS

Shannon Lush &
Jennifer Fleming

ABC
Books

The ABC 'Wave' device is a trademark of the
Australian Broadcasting Corporation and is used
under licence by HarperCollins*Publishers* Australia.

First published in 2016
by HarperCollins*Publishers* Australia Pty Limited
ABN 36 009 913 517
harpercollins.com.au

HarperCollins*Publishers*
Level 13, 201 Elizabeth Street, Sydney, NSW 2000, Australia
Unit D1, 63 Apollo Drive, Rosedale, Auckland 0632, New Zealand
A 53, Sector 57, Noida, UP, India
1 London Bridge Street, London, SE1 9GF, United Kingdom
2 Bloor Street East, 20th floor, Toronto, Ontario M4W 1A8, Canada
195 Broadway, New York, NY 10007, USA

National Library of Australia Cataloguing-in-Publication data:

Lush, Shannon, author.
Spotless pets/Shannon Lush and Jennifer Fleming.
978 0 7333 3522 8 (pbk.)
978 1 4607 0685 5 (ebook)
Includes index.
Housekeeping.
Pets – Health and hygiene.
Other creators/contributors: Fleming, Jennifer, author.
640

Cover design by HarperCollins Design Studio
Cover and internal images by shutterstock.com
Printed and bound in Australia by Griffin Press
The papers used by HarperCollins in the manufacture of this book are a natural,
recyclable product made from wood grown in sustainable plantation forests.
The fibre source and manufacturing processes meet recognised international
environmental standards, and carry certification.

CONTENTS

Introduction 1

Chapter 1 **Dogs** 5

Chapter 2 **Cats** 39

Chapter 3 **Birds** 71

Chapter 4 **Fish** 89

Chapter 5 **Horses** 101

Chapter 6 **Other Pets** 117

Chapter 7 **A-Z Stain Removal** 153

Chapter 8 **Household Formulas** 203

Appendix 1 **Quick Guide to Removing
Stains from Fabric** 209

Appendix 2 **Ideal Dog Weights** 213

Index 221

Shannon Lush is a fine arts restorer and artist who uses a range of tools, adhesives and solvents to repair items. She has a deep passion for household handy hints, with knowledge passed down through her family. For the past decade, she's solved other people's domestic disasters though regular media appearances on radio and TV, and in newspapers and the best-selling *Spotless* series of books with Jennifer Fleming, as well as *Kids Can Clean* with Erin Lush and *Stainless* with Trent Hayes. She's never been stumped by a 'how to' question around the home and loves finding creative solutions to everyday domestic problems.

Jennifer Fleming is a long-time producer and presenter at ABC Radio working on a range of popular programs. She's also a best-selling writer of several books including the number 1 selling non-fiction title of 2006, *Spotless: room-by-room solutions to domestic disasters* (with Shannon Lush). Her other books are *Speedcleaning, How to be Comfy, Save: Your money, your time, your planet, Spotless 2, Completely Spotless, Household Wisdom, Spotless A–Z* and *Spotless Baby* with Shannon Lush; *The Feel Good Body: 7 steps to easing aches and looking great* with Anna-Louise Bouvier; and *The Advertising Effect: How to change behaviour* with Adam Ferrier.

INTRODUCTION

Whether they are wild or domestic, large or small, Shannon has always loved animals and enjoyed interacting with these diverse life forms. Jennifer was lucky enough to grow up with a range of pets – from guinea pigs and chickens to cat and dogs that were all part of the family.

We love our pets. A whopping 63 per cent of Australian households own a pet and more than 83 per cent of Australians have had a pet at some time in their lives. It's almost a rite of passage for children to pester their parents for a pet.

In addition to companionship, pets offer health benefits, including lowered blood pressure. The simple act of patting your beloved pet reduces stress. You've probably heard amazing stories of pets that have saved their owners' lives. Many patients stuck in hospitals receive 'pet therapy', in which they are happily visited by a furry friend. Other unexpected benefits of owning a pet include lower infection rates because pets help strengthen children's immune systems. If you have a dog, you exercise more thanks to daily walks. In fact, most animals like to play, which increases activity levels. There's also more conversation in homes that have pets.

According to the Pet Report 2015,[1] which surveyed thousands of pet owners in the UK, a majority of owners believe pets have a positive impact on a child's development: 58 per cent said a pet makes children more responsible and 28 per cent claimed pets improved children's behaviour.

But as much as we love our pets, they are also a source of mess and stains. The most obvious and common stains are

---

1   petreport.petsathome.com

poo, pee, dirt, fur and blood. Because pets like to return to the same spot to do their business, if you don't remove every last bit of it, the area becomes a magnet for further mishaps and attractive to other animals, not to mention a source of unpleasant smells.

The good news is that pet stains can be treated with items you probably already have in your cleaning cupboard, including white vinegar, bicarb (bicarbonate of soda), a cake of bathroom soap and dishwashing liquid. Other handy items include glycerine, ultraviolet light (to detect invisible urine stains), old pantyhose, an old toothbrush and a spray pack.

When removing stains, be methodical. Don't panic and use the first product you can get your hands on. Work out the components of the stain – protein, carbohydrate, fat, chemical or biological dyes, resins or glues. **Proteins** are animal or seed based (including poo), **carbohydrates** are darker at the centre and feel stiff, **fats** are greasy between your fingers, and **resins and glues** won't dissolve in water. If you're not sure, clean with cold water first, then use hot water, then solvents. If the stain contains several components, remove proteins first with cold water, then remove fats, then any chemical or biological dyes and then any resins or glues.

Prevention is always better than cure: use mats, rugs and covers. Regardless of the stain, the sooner you deal with it, the easier it is to remove. And then reward yourself with a treat.

CHAPTER 1

DOGS

There's a reason why dogs are known as man's best friend. Whether they're working dogs or pet dogs, they are ideal companion animals and some are even treated as furry 'children'. If you own a dog, you're more likely to be active, which is good for health and wellbeing. Research has shown that children growing up in dog-owning families experience lower rates of asthma and allergies. Dogs can lift your mood and reduce loneliness, depression and stress. They are watchdogs for your home and offer protection when you're out walking. What's not to love?

WHICH DOG IS RIGHT FOR YOU?

How much is that doggie in the window, the one with the waggly tail? It's a classic song but terrible advice when deciding on a dog. Don't simply pick the most fashionable dog but the one that best matches your lifestyle. Work out the time and energy you can spend on it. If you work long hours or have limited mobility, choose a less sociable breed or factor in the cost of hiring a dog walker. If you live in an apartment, choose a low-energy breed. If you live in the bush or tick-prone areas, opt for a shorter-haired breed. Dogs bred to be non-shedding will need to be groomed more often. Consider the breed's ability to handle heat or cold, although more often in Australia it's about heat. The lighter the dog's skin, the more susceptible it will be to sun damage. Avoid buying from 'puppy farms' and consider pet rescue options. Arrange with your vet to desex, microchip and vaccinate your four-legged friend.

FEEDING

Once you've decided on a dog, talk to your vet about what it can eat, including the type of bones, because this varies according to the breed. It's likely your dog will eat a combination of tinned, dry and fresh food. If you buy commercial dog food, check that it complies with the Australian Standard: Manufacturing and Marketing of Pet Food AS 5812–2011. In addition to food, your dog needs plenty of drinking water, and this should be changed and refreshed every day.

Your dog's diet determines how you'll need to clean its poo and pee, since what goes in at one end affects what comes out at the other. While the bulk of dog food is made up of protein, there can be additives, such as caramel colouring, which leaves a brown stain that only appears a couple of days after the accident. Because caramel contains sugar, it requires an extra stage of cleaning: lightly brush with 2 drops of glycerine on an old toothbrush. Leave for 90 minutes. Dip a cake of bathroom soap in cold water and scribble it on the stain as though using a crayon. Fold a damp cloth flat and polish out the stain.

Different breeds of dog process foods differently, especially cold-weather breeds. Check with your vet. According to the RSPCA, dogs shouldn't eat any of the following:

- avocado, garlic, green unripe tomatoes, mushrooms, onions
- grapes, raisins, sultanas, currants
- fruit stones including mango seeds, apricot stones, avocado stones, fruit seeds and corncobs
- nuts including macadamia nuts (pastes such as peanut butter are fine)
- fish, cooked bones, small pieces of raw bone, fatty trimmings
- bread dough
- coffee or caffeine products
- chocolate
- Xylitol (a sugar substitute found in many foods including sugar-free chewing gum, lollies, baked goods and toothpaste)

The owners of one dog, Pluto, discovered this the hard way when he ate a macadamia nut that became caught in his bowel. The surgery cost $5000.

TIP To stop a puppy from chewing electrical cords, give it a toy. Rub the toy inside your shoes to transfer your scent and make it more appealing.

Food bowls

Think of your dog's food and water bowls in the same way as you would your dinner plate. Clean them after each use or you'll end up with a nasty, sticky, high-protein surface that's harder to clean and attracts pests. Rinse them in the sink, wash with a little dishwashing liquid and hot water, then rinse with fresh, clean water to remove soap residue. Alternatively, wipe with a small amount of salt and water, then rinse with clean water. (The salt acts as a mild abrasive.) Allow the bowls to dry after cleaning or they will quickly go mouldy.

Dogs often spill their water and food bowls and they can become contaminated with bacteria – especially during warm weather. To minimise spills, use wide-based bowls or suction-based bowls, which are more difficult to tip over. Place a plastic or rubber mat underneath bowls to make cleaning easier.

If there's both a dog and a cat in your home, keep their food bowls separate and feed them at different times. While dogs can eat most cat food, cats can't eat dog food and need higher levels of protein and fat. Cat food often contains a high proportion of fish, which can upset a dog's stomach in large volumes. Both animals have different chewing abilities: dogs' jaws move laterally and vertically, but cats' jaws only move vertically. Cats are less able to process carbohydrates because their long intestine is shorter in length. Dog saliva breaks down a multitude of bacteria. That's why a dog bite can easily become infected.

Keeping your dog cool

Dogs with heavy coats, such as a St Bernard or Siberian Husky, are not suited to the Australian climate and can suffer sunburn and heat exhaustion. There are jackets designed so you can slide fridge gels inside to keep the dog cool. Clip their hair in summer and ensure there's plenty of water for them to drink so they'll stay cool. Because dogs don't sweat, the only way they can cool down is through panting. When going for a walk, take a bowl with you so you can fill it with fresh water for your pooch. In cities, puddles are often not safe for your dog to drink from.

 To stop your dog from barking, mix 1 teaspoon of lavender oil in a 1-litre spray pack of water. Dogs don't like the smell of lavender oil. When they bark, spray the mixture under their nose. Don't look into their eyes while doing this or the dog will view it as an act of aggression.

Cleaning around feeding areas

When cleaning around dog feeding areas, only use products that are safe for pets. Avoid using bleach. It's full of harmful chemicals including dioxins and can break down surfaces, making them porous and susceptible to bacteria. Opt for non-toxic cleaning items like bicarb and white vinegar instead.

Fragrance can make dogs feel sick and cause irritation. Mark around where your dog licks with chalk and don't use insecticides and surface sprays inside the chalk line. Choose sprays that are safe for dogs.

If there are flies near the food, it could indicate you are overfeeding your dog or that the food is old. As soon as your dog finishes eating, the bowl should be cleaned. If you're busy and can't monitor your dog's food intake, use a food dispenser.

Old food can attract maggots – or fly larvae – which smell like rotten meat and can spread throughout the house. To get rid of them, vacuum and wash every surface. You'll need to clean behind and under every piece of furniture. They are active in the dark, so look for them at night with a torch and your vacuum cleaner at the ready, and clean as fast as you can. When you're finished, replace the vacuum cleaner bag. If you have a bagless vacuum cleaner, wash the dust container thoroughly.

 If using cockroach baits in the house, make sure they can't be eaten by your dog. Good locations for baits are behind the fridge and beside the oven.

 To keep dogs off the couch, tuck a bag of dried lavender behind the cushions.

Poo on carpet

Q: 'We have an elderly dog,' reports Annie. 'It walked poo up and down the hallway on cream wool Berber carpet. What do you suggest?'

Problem:	**Dog poo on carpet**
What to use:	**Plastic comb/paper towel; cake of bathroom soap, cold water, old toothbrush/pantyhose, vacuum cleaner; or bucket, cold water, dishwashing liquid, old toothbrush; glycerine**
How to apply:	Remove excess by lifting the solids with a plastic comb or by blotting liquids with paper towel. Scribble with a cake of bathroom soap dipped in cold water. If stubborn, scrub with an old toothbrush or pantyhose. Leave to dry. Vacuum.

Alternatively, remove excess then fill a bucket with cold water and enough dishwashing liquid to generate a sudsy mix. Apply only the suds with an old toothbrush, using as little water as possible. Absorb moisture by covering the area with paper towel and stand on it. Continue to change the paper towel until it's no longer wet when you stand on it.

If food is high in fats or oils (including fat from meat), remove protein first by rubbing with a cake of bathroom soap and a cold, damp cloth. To remove the fats and oils, place 2 drops of dishwashing liquid on your fingertips and massage into the stain with your fingers. Close your eyes so you can feel when the texture becomes like jelly. When this happens, the oils have become emulsified. Either wipe with a cold, damp cloth or rinse with water. Then follow either of the methods above.

If the diet is high in dry food, caramel colouring will leave a tannin-like stain. For a new or old stain, lightly brush across the surface with 2 drops of glycerine on an old toothbrush. Don't push into carpet or fabric backing or you will release tannin stains. Leave for 90 minutes. Dip a cake of bathroom soap in cold water and scribble over the stain as you would with a crayon. Fold a damp cloth flat and polish the stain out with your hand flat on the cloth. Then follow either of the methods above.

Coloured dog poo

When dogs eat vegetables, they don't break down the colourants that can cause stains. The stain removal method will depend on what the dog has been eating. To remove a beetroot stain, wipe with white vinegar on a cloth. Beta-carotenes are also removed with white vinegar on a cloth. Cheese high in cultures can irritate dogs' bowels and cause diarrhoea. Also remember that if the dog is eating several types of food, you need to remove each stain separately. Remove protein stains first with a cake of bathroom soap and cold water (hot water will set the stain). Then remove fats and oils by placing 2 drops of dishwashing liquid on your fingertips and massaging it into the stain with your fingers. Close your eyes so you can feel when the texture becomes like jelly. When this happens, the oils have become emulsified. Wipe with a cold, damp cloth.

Problem:	**Orange-coloured dog poo on carpet**
What to use:	**Cake of bathroom soap, cold water, white vinegar, cloth, sunlight/ultraviolet light, cardboard**
How to apply:	Pumpkin can be added to dogs' food to firm their stools, but it means the poo becomes very orange in colour. Scribble with a cake of bathroom soap dipped in cold water as you would with a crayon. Remove the orange stain by wiping with a cloth tightly wrung out in white vinegar. Expose to sunlight or ultraviolet light (protect areas around the stain with cardboard). Check every 2 hours until the stain has faded.

Bagging dog poo

The most environmentally friendly way to dispose of dog poo is to pick it up using a degradable plastic bag fitted over one hand like a glove. Then tie the bag up and throw it into a bin. Many councils provide free degradable plastic bags in popular parks but it's a good idea to carry a couple of spares just in case. Knot them around your dog's leash.

 TIP To stop dogs from digging in a particular area, bury their poo in the spot and they'll stay away. To encourage digging for claw health, leave bones in that spot.

Why cleaning every bit of urine is important

Dogs instinctively return to the same spot to urinate, so if pee isn't completely removed, the dog will pee there again. Not only that, but if you don't remove every last bit, there will likely be an unpleasant smell too. In some cases, you won't be able to see the stain, but you will be able to smell it.

A urine stain can spread to around twice its original size, and can even penetrate floorboards, becoming so embedded that they have to be cleaned with 'heroic methods' – above and beyond the normal. In extreme cases, the floorboards will need to be replaced. That's how pervasive urine can be.

If you can't see where the stain is, use an ultraviolet light in a darkened room. The urine will show up yellow. Mark around the stained area with white chalk so you know where to clean. Don't use bleach to remove pee stains – the ammonia in the urine will react with bleach and give off harmful fumes, and create another stain to clean.

 TIP If you see mould at the entrances to your home, mix ¼ teaspoon of oil of cloves in a 1-litre spray pack of water. Spray over the mould and doormats.

Problem:	**Fresh dog urine on carpet**
What to use:	**Ultraviolet light, white chalk, paper towel, white vinegar, old toothbrush/ cloth; glycerine**
How to apply:	In a darkened room, turn on an ultraviolet light and the urine stains will show up yellow. Mark around the yellow stains with a piece of white chalk so you can see where to clean. Absorb excess by blotting with paper towel until the towel is no longer damp. Wipe with a cloth wrung out tightly in white vinegar. Repeat if needed. Absorb moisture by covering the area with paper towel and standing on it. Continue to change the paper towel until it's no longer wet when you stand on it. If the stain isn't completely removed, lightly brush across the surface of the carpet with 2 drops of glycerine on an old toothbrush. Leave for 90 minutes. Wipe again with white vinegar and dry with paper towel. If the stain is still not removed, leave for 24 hours and wipe with white vinegar once again.

Problem: Old dog urine on carpet

What to use: Ultraviolet light, white chalk, white vinegar, cloth, paper towel; glycerine, old toothbrush

How to apply: For old stains, first find where the urine is. In a darkened room, turn on an ultraviolet light and the urine stains will show up yellow. Mark around the yellow stains with a piece of white chalk so you can see where to clean. Wipe inside the chalk marks with a cloth tightly wrung in white vinegar. Absorb moisture by covering the area with paper towel and stand on it. Continue to change the paper towel until it's no longer wet when you stand on it. If the stain isn't completely removed, lightly brush across the surface of the carpet with 2 drops of glycerine on an old toothbrush. Leave for 90 minutes. Wipe again with white vinegar and dry with paper towel. If the stain is still not removed, leave for 24 hours and wipe with white vinegar once again.

 TIP If your dog has long hair, protect against ticks by clipping hair on its underside.

General spot cleaner for carpet

Don't use enzyme-based cleaners for spot cleaning. Instead, mix 2 tablespoons of bicarb, 2 tablespoons of white vinegar, 2 tablespoons of methylated spirits, 2 teaspoons of glycerine, 2 teaspoons of eucalyptus oil, 2 teaspoons of dishwashing liquid and 1 litre of water in a spray pack. Lightly mist over the stain on the carpet, then wipe with a damp cloth.

Discoloured carpet

Dog (and cat) urine can affect dye chemicals used in some carpets. This causes discoloration, bleaching or dye run. Once the carpet is bleached, it can be patched (see page 53) or re-dyed (see page 99).

Problem: Dog urine on stone/timber

What to use: White vinegar, cloth, plaster of Paris, water, brush

How to apply: Wipe with white vinegar on a cloth. If stubborn, mix plaster of Paris and water to the consistency of peanut butter. To each cup of mixture, add 2 teaspoons of white vinegar. Spread 6 mm to 1.3 cm thick over the stain. Allow to dry completely. If it feels cold on the back of your hand, it's not dry. When dry, crack it with the back of the brush and brush away.

DID YOU KNOW? Research from the University of Adelaide suggests left-pawed dogs are more aggressive to strangers than their right-pawed counterparts. There's an even number of left-pawed and right-pawed dogs.

 TIP To stop a puppy from chewing on wooden furniture, wipe over the timber with 2 drops of either lavender oil, cinnamon oil, chilli oil or oil of cloves on a cloth.

Problem: Dog urine soaked into timber

What to use: Plaster of Paris, water, white vinegar, brush; or black teabags, white vinegar, bucket, hot water, cloth

How to apply: If urine soaks into timber, it's difficult to remove. Mix plaster of Paris and water to the consistency of peanut butter. To each cup of mixture, add 2 teaspoons of white vinegar. Spread 6 mm to 1.3 cm thick over the stain. If you have access underneath the floorboards, apply to both sides of the timber. Allow to dry completely. If it feels cold on the back of your hand, it's not dry. When dry, crack it with the back of a brush and sweep away. You may have to use this technique every day for up to a week. In the worst cases, when urine has been there for years, you'll have to replace the floorboards.

If the floors are coated in polyurethane and it's scratched, urine can penetrate through the scratches. To clean, mix 4 black teabags and ½ cup of white vinegar per bucket of hot water. Wipe this mixture over the surface with a cloth.

TIP To deter dogs, for hard surfaces wipe with a little lavender oil on a cloth. For absorbent surfaces, mix 1 teaspoon of lavender oil and 1 litre of water in a spray pack and lightly mist over the area.

Problem:	**Dog vomit on carpet**
What to use:	**Plastic comb/paper towel, cake of bathroom soap, cold water, dishwashing liquid, cloth; or glycerine, old toothbrush, cake of bathroom soap, cloth; paper towel**
How to apply:	Remove excess by lifting the solids with a plastic comb or blotting liquids with paper towel. Scribble with a cake of bathroom soap dipped in cold water as you would with a crayon. Massage with 2 drops of dishwashing liquid on your fingertips until the liquid feels like jelly. Wipe with a damp cloth until the dishwashing liquid is removed. If the vomit is a caramel colour, lightly brush across the surface of the carpet with 2 drops of glycerine on an old toothbrush. Leave for 90 minutes. Scribble with a cake of bathroom soap dipped in cold water as you would with a crayon. Fold a damp cloth flat and polish the stain out. In all cases, absorb moisture by covering the area with paper towel and standing on it. Continue to change the paper towel until it's no longer wet when you stand on it. When

almost dry, repeat the whole process. If a shadow mark appears after a couple of weeks, repeat again.

Dealing with dog saliva

Dog drool has incredible properties. The University of Arizona is even researching whether it contains probiotics (healthy bacteria). But dog saliva on your couch or car window can be a challenge to remove. It's so powerful it can strip the top layer of car window tinting, etch glass or damage the duco on your car. Remove saliva as soon as possible with soapy water. If the glass is permanently etched, wipe with white vinegar then rub with sweet almond oil. Reapply as needed.

For the car exterior, wash with a cake of bathroom soap and water, and polish with a cutting compound (use a proprietary product, or make your own by mixing equal parts glycerine and talcum powder) using tightly rolled pantyhose. The cutting compound won't damage the duco but can be time-consuming to apply. To speed up the process, apply using a sheepskin buff. Wipe with leather conditioner. Make your own by placing 1 teaspoon of beeswax, 1 teaspoon of lavender oil and 1 teaspoon of lemon oil on a 100 per cent cotton cloth, such as an old T-shirt. Place in the microwave in a microwave-safe dish. Microwave on high in 10-second bursts until the beeswax melts. After using the cloth, place it in a zip-lock bag and store in the freezer ready to use again.

One danger area is dog saliva on the couch. It's difficult to remove and damages the surface of leather.

Problem: Dog saliva on fabric couch

What to use: Steam cleaner, carpet cleaning chemicals, bicarb, white vinegar, methylated spirits, glycerine, eucalyptus oil

How to apply: Steam cleaners can be hired at the supermarket and come with a bottle of carpet cleaning chemicals. Use half the quantity of carpet cleaning chemicals and add 2 tablespoons of bicarb, 2 tablespoons of white vinegar, 2 tablespoons of methylated spirits, 2 teaspoons of glycerine and 2 teaspoons of eucalyptus oil. Use the upholstery arm of the steam cleaner and steam clean the entire panel, not just the stained area. Repeat on empty to draw out moisture.

Problem: Dog saliva on leather couch

What to use: Bead of water, walnut/coloured shoe cream, cloth, stainless-steel spoon, boiling water, tea towel, leather conditioner

How to apply: Before tackling any stains, work out if the leather is waxed, plasticised or oiled. Place a single bead of water on an inconspicuous part of the leather. If the water soaks in slowly, it's waxed. If the water rolls off, the leather coating is plasticised. If the water soaks straight into the leather, it's oiled. For brown leather, cut a walnut (the nut, not the shell) in half and rub the cut surface over the area. Leave for 1 hour for the colour to cure. For other leather, use shoe cream (not shoe polish or wax) that matches the colour of the leather. Apply with a cloth over the marked area only. To set the shoe cream, rub over it with the back of a warm stainless-steel spoon (dip the spoon in a glass of boiling water and dry with a tea towel). Wipe with leather conditioner. Make your own by placing 1 teaspoon of beeswax, 1 teaspoon of lavender oil and 1 teaspoon of lemon oil on a 100 per cent cotton cloth, such as an old T-shirt. Place in the microwave in a microwave-safe dish. Microwave on high in 10-second bursts until the beeswax melts. After using the cloth, place it in a zip-lock bag and store in the freezer ready to use again.

GROOMING AND HEALTH

Create hygienic resting and sleeping areas for your dog. One option is a dog sling or hammock in canvas or shade cloth that provides airflow. These can be washed in the washing machine. If made of rubber, clean with dishwashing liquid and water. If your dog insists on sitting on the couch, put down an old towel, blanket or sheet. If your dog wanders all over the house, vacuum often and wipe with disposable rubber gloves to keep hair under control. For a large area, put washed disposable rubber gloves on your feet and walk over the carpet.

The rubber glove technique

To remove pet hair from furniture and carpet, put disposable rubber gloves on your hands and wash the gloves with a cake of bathroom soap and cold water. Shake them dry. Stroke them over the upholstery or carpet. The static charge and drag of the rubber pulls the hair into a ball that can be easily picked up and placed in the bin. It works exceptionally well on clothing too, so you needn't look like a lamington. Stroke your dog with gloved hands to remove loose hairs.

DID YOU KNOW? Poodle wool, or chiengora, can be used for knitting. You could sell the wool to cover the cost of grooming. One company, Woofspun, converts your dog hair into jumpers and scarves. There's even a book titled *Knitting with Dog Hair: Better a sweater from a dog you know and love than from a sheep you'll never meet* (St Martin's Griffin, 1997). To clean the hair, boil a pot of water on the stove, place an open-weave cloth, preferably cotton or linen, over the top of the pot and lay the hair on top of the cloth. The steam will clean the hair and compact it, making it easier to spin.

Brushing your dog

The more often you groom your dog, the better. Everyone in the family should be involved. The type of brush to use – nylon, wire or bristle – will depend on its coat and what it likes. Some dogs like sharp bristles while others don't. Wire brushes are good for long-haired dogs with fleas, but don't use the brush near their head because the wires can aggravate their nose and eyes. After using a wire brush, wash and dry it or it will go rusty. Bristle brushes are easy to wash and use. Be careful with nylon brushes – don't brush too quickly because it can cause static charge that will matt their hair. Slowly move it through their coat. While brushing, check the coat for ticks and fleas.

Washing your dog

Wash your dog once a week, even if it's only a dry bath. If you smell the dog's brush and it stinks, it's time to wash the dog. Small dogs can be washed in the laundry sink. For a large dog, buy a children's shell sandpit. If your dog scratches its coat, add rosemary tea to the wash. Mix 8 teaspoons of dried rosemary or 16 teaspoons of fresh rosemary into 4 cups of boiling water. Allow it to steep. Add 2 teaspoons of this mixture to the wash water. If your dog has eczema, add fresh or dried mint – not peppermint – to the wash water. For silky dogs, add maidenhair fern to the wash water. After bathing, towel your dog as soon as possible or you'll be cleaning wet hair from your walls. Cotton towels have the best absorbency.

A dry bath for a dog

As dogs grow older, they can't shed their skin as easily, making them smellier, so exfoliation is important. Most dogs love a dry bath. It can be a bit messy, so do it outside. Mix unprocessed wheat bran and white vinegar until the mixture resembles breadcrumbs, and brush it through the dog's coat. To inhibit fleas, add mint sauce to the mix. This also relieves eczema. Dogs love the smell of mint, so it's like a puppy day spa for them.

If your dog scratches its ears, it could be from black mite, which looks like black dirt. Put a small amount of baby oil onto a cotton ball and wipe it in their ear. This gets rid of the mite because it can't adhere to the surface of the ear. Wipe your dog's ears on a regular basis.

For flyblown ears, put 1 drop of lavender oil on your fingertips and massage it into the tops of their ears. Even though dogs don't like the smell of lavender oil, it's preferable to flies. Alternatively, spray mint tea over their ears.

Clean dog paws by placing damp old socks on your dog's feet and letting it run around. The socks will clean its paws as it runs.

Rolling in soil

Q: 'My dog loves to roll in soil,' says James. 'What's the best way to clean him?'

Problem:	**Dog covered in decomposed soil**
What to use:	**Dog shampoo, warm water, cake of bathroom soap**
How to apply:	Dogs love rolling in decomposed soil where animals have died because the scent indicates to other dogs that they are tough. Wash with dog shampoo then wash in warm water with a cake of bathroom soap. Don't use gels.

 Most dogs love to swim. While the science is inconclusive, there's a widely held view that ocean-swimming dogs attract sharks because of their thrashing action in the water. Whether they've been swimming in salt or chlorinated water, rinse them with fresh water afterwards.

Cleaning your dog's teeth

Keep your dog's teeth clean by giving it large bones to chew on. Dogs can't eat cooked bones because they can splinter. As dogs age, they can develop black tartar around their teeth. When this happens, use charcoal chews or charcoal on an old toothbrush, or consult your vet.

Clipping your dog's claws

Dogs that live inside the house need their claws to be regularly clipped. One option is to secure a piece of sandpaper that they can scratch on to a board near their bathroom box. Another option is to use nail clippers designed for your breed of dog.

Problem: **Scratch marks on leather**

What to use: **Bead of water, walnut/coloured shoe cream, cloth, stainless-steel spoon, boiling water, tea towel, leather conditioner**

How to apply: Before tackling any stains, work out if the leather is waxed, plasticised or oiled. Place a single bead of water on an inconspicuous part of the leather. If the water soaks in slowly, it's waxed. If the water rolls off, the leather coating is plasticised. If the water soaks straight into the leather, it's oiled. For brown leather, cut a walnut (the nut, not the shell) in half and rub the cut surface over the area. Leave for 1 hour for the colour to cure. For other leather, use shoe cream (not shoe polish or wax) that matches the colour of the leather. Apply with a cloth over the marked area only. To set the shoe cream, rub over it with the back of a warm stainless-steel spoon (dip the spoon in a glass of boiling water and dry with a tea towel). Wipe with leather conditioner. Make your own by placing 1 teaspoon of beeswax, 1 teaspoon of lavender oil and 1 teaspoon of lemon oil on a 100 per cent cotton cloth, such as an old T-shirt. Place in the microwave in a microwave-safe dish. Microwave on high in

10-second bursts until the beeswax melts. After using the cloth, place it in a zip-lock bag and store in the freezer ready to use again.

Problem: **Blood on carpet**

What to use: **Cake of bathroom soap, cold water, old toothbrush, cloth, paper towel; white vinegar; glycerine; unprocessed wheat bran**

How to apply: Scribble over the stain with a cake of bathroom soap dipped in cold water as you would with a crayon. Scrub with an old toothbrush in every direction – north, south, east and west. Wipe with a cold, damp cloth. Absorb moisture by covering the area with paper towel and standing on it. Continue to change the paper towel until it's no longer wet when you stand on it.

If you tried to remove the blood with a foam upholstery cleaner or commercial spray product, neutralise first by wiping with a cloth tightly wrung out in white vinegar; if you used liquid carpet cleaner, neutralise first by brushing with unprocessed wheat bran. When neutralised, place 2 drops of glycerine on an old toothbrush and lightly brush across the surface of the carpet. Leave for 90 minutes then follow the steps described above.

Problem: Oily marks on upholstery

What to use: Unprocessed wheat bran, bowl, white vinegar, dishwashing liquid, pantyhose, spray pack/cloth, hairspray

How to apply: Because dogs don't sweat, there's a lot of oil in their coats. If not regularly washed, they can leave dark marks when they rub up against furniture or curtains. It's a tough oil to get rid of. To remove, place 1 cup of unprocessed wheat bran in a large bowl. Add drops of white vinegar one at a time, stirring as you go, until the mixture resembles breadcrumbs. It shouldn't be wet. Add ½ teaspoon of dishwashing liquid to the mixture. Then place the mixture into the toe of a pair of pantyhose and tie up tightly. It should be the size of a tennis ball. Lightly mist the area to be cleaned with water from a spray pack (on the mist setting) or wipe with a cloth that is damp but not wet. Brush the pantyhose across the damp surface. It's likely the dog will return to this spot, so protect it by spraying with hairspray. It will make cleaning easier next time.

 TIP It's common for Silky Terriers and Shih Tzu breeds to have tear stains around their eyes. To remove, wipe with glycerine on a cotton bud, leave for 10 minutes, then wipe with dry cotton ball. To remove stains from their coat, add 2 drops of glycerine to their bath water.

Cleaning collars and harnesses

If the collar or harness is made of nylon or polycotton, wet
with dishwashing liquid and warm water. Then, standing over
a sink, wrap it around a pen in a spiral pattern and hold the
end with 1 thumb. Release your thumb and pull the other end.
As it twists around the pencil, the dirt and water will flick off.
Repeat until all the water is removed. If the collar or harness
is made of leather, rub with saddle soap and pantyhose until
clean. Remove excess saddle soap by wiping over it with damp
pantyhose. Dry in the shade so it doesn't go stiff. If it has
metal-backed studs, dry it quickly because the metal can rust.
Saliva can also cause buckles to rust, so clean them as soon as
possible. Hang leads out of reach, except in the case of guide
dogs, when easy access is important.

Ticks

'Freeze it, don't squeeze it' is the latest advice. Apply a spray
that contains ether, such as Wart-Off or Medi Freeze Skin
Tag Remover. Place the nozzle over the tick, spray it and wait
10 minutes for the tick to die. Once it's dead, you can brush
it off.[2] If in doubt, or if there are signs of toxicity, see the vet
immediately. If you live in a tick-prone area, your vet will have
medication available.

---

2   www.abc.net.au/catalyst/stories/4177191.htm

Fleas

Fleas don't like mint, particularly pennyroyal and Persian mint. If there's a pregnant woman or pet in the house, use Persian mint, which is available as a low-growing plant from nurseries. Crush 1 tablespoon of fresh Persian mint in a mortar and pestle and steep it in 1 tablespoon of methylated spirits. Add 1 litre of boiling water. Strain the mixture and mist over the kennel every 9 days.

Alternatively, mix ¼ teaspoon of oil of pennyroyal in 1 litre of water. Every 9 days, mist over a flea-infested kennel. Put on a pair of disposable rubber gloves and place 1 to 2 drops of oil of pennyroyal in the palm of your hand. Rub your hands together and pat the dog from head to tail. If it's reluctant, wait until it's sleeping and place a drop on the back of its neck between its shoulder blades.

⚠ WARNING

Don't use oil of pennyroyal if the dog or women in the house are pregnant.

Another alternative is to take 4 teaspoons of dried mint or 8 teaspoons of freshly chopped mint and leave to steep in 1 litre of boiling water. Strain the mixture. Lightly spray the flea-infested area once a day for a month. Add 1 cup of this mixture to a dog's bath. This also helps with itches and scratches – dogs love it.

Dry nose

If your dog's nose is dry, wipe with a little petroleum jelly (Vaseline). Don't use too much because if the dog licks it, it could cause diarrhoea. For ongoing problems, see your vet.

> **Problem:** **Petroleum jelly (Vaseline) on carpet**
> **What to use:** **Dishwashing liquid, cloth, paper towel**
> **How to apply:** Massage stain with 2 drops of dishwashing liquid on your fingertips until it feels like jelly. Wipe with a damp cloth until the dishwashing liquid is removed. Absorb moisture by covering the area with paper towel and standing on it. Continue changing the paper towel until it's no longer wet when you stand on it.

Ideal dog weights

See Appendix 2 on page 213 to find out the healthy weight range for your dog's breed.

 TIP If burying your pet in the backyard, ensure the hole is deep. Don't wrap the body in plastic because it needs to break down.

SLEEP, PLAY AND TRAVEL

Most modern dog beds have removable covers that can be cleaned in the washing machine. Air the dog's bed or mattress each day by standing it against a wall. If you can, place both sides in sunshine. Use a cover with a tight weave so ticks and fleas can't penetrate.

Wash blankets and old towels in the washing machine with cheap hair shampoo and 2 drops of tea tree oil to sterilise. Freshen bedding by adding 1 teaspoon of eucalyptus oil to the wash. It removes odours and can help deter fleas and ticks.

Dog beanbag beds are covered in an open nylon mesh that can be washed in the washing machine and hung on the clothesline. Alternatively, hang the beanbag on the clothesline and hose it.

If there are fleas, add mint tea to the washing water. To make mint tea, add 2 teaspoons of dried mint or 4 teaspoons of fresh mint to 240 ml of hot water. Allow the tea to steep for 15 minutes then strain. Spray the bedding with mint tea.

 Keep a dog mat at the entrance of your house to reduce the amount of dirt tracked through the house.

Dog kennels

Dog kennels are made of timber or plastic. To clean, remove the contents of the kennel and wipe the interior with white vinegar on a cloth. Then wipe with a cake of bathroom soap and water. To remove the smell, mix ¼ teaspoon of oil of cloves, 2 tablespoons of dried mint and 1 litre of hot water in a spray pack. Allow to cool. Spray over every surface and wipe with pantyhose. The oil of cloves kills mould and the mint kills fleas. Reapply once a month.

Portable kennels are made of powder-coated steel and polyester fabric. Wash the fabric with a cake of bathroom soap and cold water. Dog kennels should be elevated so air can circulate. One option is to place bricks underneath the kennel.

If you live in an apartment, you might also have a pet loo or potty patch. This contraption has a porous synthetic grass mat on top of a plastic urine collection tray. The best way to clean it is to spray with white vinegar and water and rinse with fresh water.

Dog toys

Cleaning squeaky toys:
- Mix ¼ teaspoon of tea tree oil and 1 litre of water in a spray pack. Tea tree oil is a great disinfectant and is non-toxic.
- Spray over the toy and wipe with a cloth.
- To clean a mouldy rubber toy, add ¼ teaspoon of oil of cloves to a 4-litre bucket of blood-heat (body temperature) water.
- Place the toy in the bucket, squeeze so water gets inside and leave for 2 hours.
- Remove, squeeze out the water and set aside to dry.

Cleaning fabric toys:
- Wash separately in the washing machine in a pillowcase or delicates bag.

Tennis balls:
- Saliva sticks to the fluff on a tennis ball, so once your dog has caught the ball in its mouth, wherever the ball bounces

has to be cleaned. It's much better to use a smooth ball than a hairy one. If you have a ball thrower, you don't have to touch the ball either.

Travelling with dogs

- Keep a dedicated blanket on the car seat with a waterproof sheet underneath.
- Before a long journey, take your dog for a walk first. During the journey, stop regularly – each hour is recommended because dog bladders are smaller than human bladders. You'll have a cleaner car and a less stressed animal.
- Never leave your dog in a parked car.
- Bring a supply of food and water with you in the car.
- Carry paper towels and disinfectant to clean up any mishaps.
- If your dog moves around, consider using a dog restraint inside the car.
- Clean up dog poo as soon as possible.

Problem:	**Dog vomit in the car**
What to use:	**Plastic comb/paper towel, cake of bathroom soap, cold water, cloth, dishwashing liquid; glycerine, old toothbrush, lemon juice, spray pack; unprocessed wheat bran, bowl, white vinegar, pantyhose**
How to apply:	Remove excess by lifting the solids with a plastic comb or blotting liquids with paper towel. Scribble with a cake of bathroom

soap dipped in cold water as you would with a crayon. Rub with a damp cloth. Massage with 2 drops of dishwashing liquid on your fingertips until the liquid feels like jelly. Wipe with a damp cloth until the dishwashing liquid is removed.

If the vomit is a caramel colour, remove excess then lightly brush across the surface with 2 drops of glycerine on an old toothbrush. Leave for 90 minutes. Scribble with a cake of bathroom soap dipped in cold water as you would with a crayon. Fold a damp cloth flat and polish the stain out. Absorb moisture with paper towel. When almost dry, repeat. If a shadow returns in a couple of weeks, repeat again. To remove the smell, mix 1 tablespoon of lemon juice with 1 litre of water in a spray pack and spray over the area.

If there's a watermark, place 1 cup of unprocessed wheat bran in a large bowl. Add drops of white vinegar one at a time, stirring as you go, until the mixture resembles breadcrumbs. It shouldn't be wet. Place the mixture into the toe of a pair of pantyhose and tie up tightly. It will be the size of a tennis ball. Rub over the stain until removed.

How to deal with dog smell in cars

The smell is from the oil in their coat and means your dog needs a bath. Keep an old blanket for them to sit on in the car. To remove the oily stain, place 1 cup of unprocessed wheat bran in a large bowl. Add drops of white vinegar one at a time, stirring as you go, until the mixture resembles breadcrumbs. It shouldn't be wet. Mix in 2 drops of dishwashing liquid. Place the mixture into the toe of pantyhose and tie up tightly. It will be the size of a tennis ball. Rub over the area. Don't forget to wipe over doors and windows.

CHAPTER 2

CATS

If we didn't have cats, what would we watch on YouTube? These owners of nine lives were treated as semi-divine in Egyptian times and they haven't forgotten it. Felines have inspired global empires such as Hello Kitty and the popular musical *Cats*. And let's not forget cat cafes that allow you to cuddle up to a cat while drinking coffee. Cats are curious by nature, leading them into potentially tricky situations – up trees, for example. Even though they often pretend not to need you, they do.

IS A CAT RIGHT FOR YOU?

Before you decide to get a cat, make sure you and members of your family are not allergic. If you pass that hurdle, the next step is to work out what breed of cat best suits you. A long-haired cat will need more time for grooming or could end up with fur balls. If you are time-poor, opt for a short-haired cat. Another consideration is your home. If you live in a high-rise apartment with a balcony, you'll need to create a barrier so that the cat can't climb over or around the balcony.

Buy a cat collar and include your name and contact details on it, and update it if you change address. Also on the checklist are vaccinations, desexing and microchipping – your vet will keep these details on file for you.

FEEDING

The amount of food your cat needs will depend on its age and activity level. Most should be fed twice a day with a combination of wet and dry food. Because cats can be fussy eaters, you may need to try several brands of food before you find a good match. If in doubt, consult your vet. As with dogs, your cat's diet determines how you'll need to clean its poo and pee, since what goes in at one end affects what comes out at the other. Cats eat animal-based proteins and fats, so the standard stain removal technique is to use a cake of bathroom soap and cold water. If the food contains fish, it may have a higher oil content, requiring an additional stage of cleaning with 2 drops of dishwashing liquid emulsified into the stain with your fingers then wiped off with a damp cloth.

Food bowls

Choose a cat bowl made of metal, ceramic or glass. Plastic tends to hold smells that cats don't like. Clean the bowl in the sink after each meal with dishwashing liquid and hot water. Rinse and dry before reusing. Locate the feeding bowl away from kitty litter, with a mat placed underneath to catch spills. Keep several bowls – that way there's always a clean one ready for use.

As mentioned in the chapter on dogs, if you have both a dog and a cat, keep their food bowls separate and feed them at different times. While dogs can eat most cat food, cats can't eat dog food and need higher levels of protein and fat from meat. Cat food is often high in fish, which can upset a dog's stomach in large volumes. Dog jaws move laterally and vertically but cat jaws only move vertically. Cats are less able to process carbohydrates because their long intestine is shorter in length.

Cats need to drink plenty of water so make sure their water bowl is filled regularly. If your cat tips its water bowl over or won't drink, consider a water fountain.

 Many house cats don't get enough exercise and put on weight. If your cat is overweight, increase its activity levels by giving it toys to chase. Add cooked beetroot, sweet potato and carrot to its food for dietary fibre that slows digestion. To remove stains created by these vegetables, wipe with white vinegar on a cloth.

Curious cats

Many cats are inquisitive and want to see what's on kitchen bench tops. If there's nothing to hold their interest, they'll move away. But because most cats have a short memory, they'll come back to check out what's on the bench top again and again. Close kitchen doors if possible. Cats will even lick a cold barbecue so keep the cover shut when not in use. Keep a lid on butter – cats love it. To deter cats, mix 1 mothball, 1 teaspoon of naphthalene flakes or 1 teaspoon of Vicks VapoRub with 1 litre of water in a spray pack. Shake well. Mist around areas where you have trouble with cats. Wipe Vicks VapoRub around door frames. Scatter naphthalene flakes under the house. To ameliorate the smell of naphthalene, sprinkle lemon thyme nearby.

⚠ WARNING

Be careful using mothballs or naphthalene flakes if you have children under 3 years of age. It's toxic if eaten. Some mothballs contain camphor, which can bleach carpet if overused, so only apply as described.

 TIP Don't leave clean laundry lying around – cats will sleep on top of it. Instead, throw a sheet over the top of the washing. Cats also love lying in bathtubs. In case the cat has been there, clean the bath with lavender mix (see page 206) and water before using.

Kitty litter

Cats return to the same spot to do their business and training is fairly straightforward. There are many types of trays, boxes and brands of litter available. Ensure the tray is deep or you'll have litter everywhere. If the tray isn't deep enough, glue door brush (available at hardware stores) around the top edge of the tray to catch the litter. Place the tray in a private and quiet area. Cats hate using dirty litter boxes, so remove soiled litter as soon as the cat has used the tray and change the litter regularly. Wash the box each week with hot soapy water. If the kitty litter smells, remove it, pour ½ cm of white vinegar into the empty litter box, let the white vinegar stand for 20 minutes then rinse with cold water. Cats can spray their pee up to 3 metres away. If there's an odour near the kitty litter, it could be from invisible spray. Wash the area around the tray with white vinegar to neutralise and eradicate smells. To protect walls, attach disposable aluminium stovetop splatter guards along 3 sides of the litter tray.

My cat won't use the litter tray

If your cat doesn't use the litter tray, it might need training. When the cat poos, place the litter tray near the poo. Cats like to poo in the same spot. Gradually move the litter tray to the desired area. Check there's sufficient litter or they won't use it. As seen in the movie *Meet the Parents*, you can even train a cat to use the toilet.

Pregnant women should avoid cleaning cat litter trays because of a harmful parasite in cat's faeces that can cause toxoplasmosis. If you can't avoid it, wear disposable rubber gloves and a dust mask when cleaning cat litter trays and wash your hands thoroughly afterwards. If you have an outdoor cat, wear gloves and use tools when gardening.

Problem: **Cat poo on carpet**

What to use: **Plastic comb, cake of bathroom soap, cold water, pantyhose, paper towel; talcum powder, cardboard**

How to apply: Remove solids by lifting with a plastic comb. Scribble with a cake of bathroom soap dipped in cold water as though using a crayon. Rub with damp rolled-up pantyhose in all directions – north, south, east and west. Absorb moisture by covering the area with paper towel and standing on it. Continue to change the paper towel until it's no longer wet when you stand on it. If the stain is very wet, remove excess poo and sprinkle with talcum powder to dry the area. To stop the mess from spreading while cleaning, hold a piece of stiff cardboard flat against the carpet as you would a dustpan and broom. Then follow the steps above.

Why cleaning every bit of urine is important

Like dogs, cats instinctively return to the same spot to urinate, so if pee isn't removed entirely, the cat will pee there again. That's why you must remove every bit of urine when cleaning. Not only that, but if you don't remove every last bit, there will likely be an unpleasant smell too. You may not be able to see the stain, but you will be able to smell it. When it rains, the smell of cat urine can return and means the urine wasn't completely removed when cleaned.

Urine can spread to around twice the size of the original mark and can even penetrate through floorboards, becoming so embedded that they have to be cleaned with 'heroic methods' – above and beyond the normal. In extreme cases, the floorboards will need to be replaced. That's how pervasive it can be. If you can't see where the stain is, use an ultraviolet light in a darkened room. The urine will show up yellow.

Avoid using bleach to clean cat urine – the ammonia in the urine will react with the bleach and give off harmful fumes, won't remove the urine and will create a new stain. Avoid using enzyme-based cleaners for spot cleaning. Instead, mix 2 tablespoons of bicarb, 2 tablespoons of white vinegar, 2 tablespoons of methylated spirits, 2 teaspoons of glycerine, 2 teaspoons of eucalyptus oil, 2 teaspoons of dishwashing liquid and 1 litre of water in a spray pack. Lightly mist over carpet, then rub with a rolled-up pair of pantyhose.

Problem: **Cat urine on carpet**

What to use: **Ultraviolet light, white chalk, paper towel, white vinegar, cloth**

How to apply: If you can't see the stain in a darkened room, turn on an ultraviolet light and the urine stains will show up yellow. Mark around the yellow stains with a piece of white chalk so you know where to clean. Remove excess by blotting with paper towel. Place white vinegar on a cloth and wring tightly so it's damp but not wet. Rub from the outside to the inside of the stain. Absorb moisture by covering the area with paper towel and standing on it. Continue to change the paper towel until it's no longer wet when you stand on it. You'll need to remove every bit of urine or the smell will linger.

Problem: **Cat urine on stone (not marble or limestone)**

What to use: **White vinegar, cloth; plaster of Paris, water, brush; soap flakes/cake of bathroom soap**

How to apply: Wipe with white vinegar on a cloth. If stubborn, mix plaster of Paris and water to the consistency of peanut butter. To each cup of mixture, add 2 teaspoons of white vinegar. Spread 6 mm to 1.3 cm thick over the stain. Allow to dry completely. If it feels cold on the back of your hand, it's not dry. When dry, crack it with the back of a brush and brush away. Don't use white vinegar on marble or limestone. Instead, add 1 teaspoon of soap flakes (or a grated cake of bathroom soap) to the plaster of Paris mix.

Problem: **Fresh cat urine on timber**
What to use: **Paper towel, white vinegar, cloth**
How to apply: Remove excess by blotting with paper towel. Place white vinegar on a cloth and wring tightly so it's damp but not wet. Blot over the mark.

Problem: **Old cat urine on timber**
What to use: **Ultraviolet light, white chalk, white vinegar; plaster of Paris, water, brush**
How to apply: First, find where the urine is. In a darkened room, turn on an ultraviolet light and the urine stains will show up yellow. Mark around the yellow stains with a piece of white chalk so you can see where to clean. Wipe inside the chalk marks with a cloth tightly wrung in white vinegar. If the urine has soaked through the floorboard grooves, mix plaster of Paris and water to the consistency of peanut butter. For every cup of paste, add 2 teaspoons of white vinegar. Spread 6 mm to 1.3 cm thick over the floorboards. Allow to dry completely.

If it feels cold on the back of your hand, it's not dry. When dry, crack it with the back of a brush and brush away.

Problem: **Cat urine on mattress**

What to use: **Paper towel, ultraviolet light, white chalk, white vinegar, cloth; hot white vinegar**

How to apply: Remove excess by blotting with paper towel. In a darkened room, turn on an ultraviolet light and the urine stains will show up yellow. Mark around the yellow stains with a piece of white chalk so you can see where to clean. Place white vinegar on a cloth and wring tightly so it's damp but not wet. Work from the outside to the inside of the stain. Absorb moisture by covering the area with paper towel and standing on it. Continue to change the paper towel until it's no longer wet when you stand on it. You need to remove every bit of urine or the smell will linger. Check after 48 hours. If the urine has soaked through the mattress, take the mattress outside and pour hot white vinegar through the stain again and again until the smell is gone. Allow to dry. If it still smells, repeat.

Problem: **Cat urine on unsealed terracotta**
What to use: **Plaster of Paris, water, white vinegar, ultraviolet light, white chalk, brush**
How to apply: Terracotta is very absorbent. Mix plaster of Paris and water to the consistency of peanut butter. For every cup of paste, add 2 tablespoons of white vinegar. In a darkened room, turn on an ultraviolet light and the urine stains will show up yellow. Mark around the yellow stains with a piece of white chalk so you can see where to clean. Place the plaster of Paris mixture over the stain 6 mm to 1.3 cm thick and leave for 24 hours. Allow to dry completely. If it feels cold on the back of your hand, it's not dry. When dry, crack it with the back of a brush and brush away.

 To seal terracotta tiles, mix ½ cup of PVA glue with 1 cup of just-warm water. Sweep over the surface in even, parallel lines using a clean, soft kitchen broom. Leave the tiles to dry. Clean the broom immediately by massaging with dishwashing liquid and warm water. To remove the seal, scrub with a stiff broom and boiling water.

Vomit on carpet

Q: 'My problem is with a cat that throws up,' says Debbie. 'The cat food is brightly coloured and stains the carpet immediately. What should I do?'

Problem: Coloured cat vomit on carpet

What to use: Plastic comb/paper towel, cake of bathroom soap, water, cloth, paper towel; glycerine, old toothbrush

How to apply: The colour is from caramel used in some cat food, which leaves a tannin-like stain. Clean quickly. Remove excess by lifting the solids with a plastic comb or blotting liquids with paper towel. Scribble with a cake of bathroom soap dipped in cold water as you would with a crayon. Fold a damp cloth flat and polish the stain out. Absorb moisture by covering the area with paper towel and standing on it. Continue to change the paper towel until it's no longer wet when you stand on it. If a stain remains, lightly brush across the surface with 2 drops of glycerine on an old toothbrush and leave for 90 minutes. When almost dry, repeat the glycerine application. If a shadow returns in a couple of weeks, repeat.

Urine on curtains

Q: 'My cat sprayed on brand-new, rubber-backed cotton curtains,' reports Chris. 'What should I do?'

Problem: Cat urine on curtains

What to use: White vinegar, cloth, Vicks VapoRub/ naphthalene flakes/mothballs, spray pack

How to apply: If the curtains can be washed, wash in the washing machine adding ½ cup of white vinegar to the wash water. If the curtains can't be washed, wipe with white vinegar on a cloth. Be aware that cat urine can affect the adhesive bond between the curtain fabric and the lining. To deter cats, lightly mist with 1 teaspoon of Vicks VapoRub, 1 teaspoon of naphthalene flakes or 2 mothballs in a 1-litre spray pack of water.

Problem: **Cat urine spraying or marking upholstery**
What to use: **Cloth, white vinegar, paper towel**
How to apply: Wipe with a cloth tightly wrung in white vinegar. Absorb moisture by covering the area with paper towel and standing on it. Continue to change the paper towel until it's no longer wet when you stand on it. Remove every bit of urine or the smell will linger.

Problem: **Cat saliva on fabric**
What to use: **Lavender oil, water, spray pack, cloth**
How to apply: Cat saliva has an organic deposit in which bacteria can grow and some diseases can be spread, so it's best to remove it. Mix 1 teaspoon of lavender oil per 1 litre of water in a spray pack. Spray over the saliva and wipe with a cloth.

Discoloured carpet

Cat (and dog) urine can affect dye chemicals used in some carpets. This causes discoloration, bleaching or dye run. Once the carpet is bleached, it can be patched (see below) or re-dyed (see page 99).

How to patch carpet

- Cut around the damaged part of the carpet with a Stanley knife to create a neat shape.
- Find a piece of matching carpet that's slightly larger than the stained area (from inside a cupboard or an old sample from a carpet store). Make sure the pattern is going in the same direction.
- Make a paper template of the cut-out piece of carpet.
- Transfer the template to the piece of patch carpet and cut the patch carpet around the template with a sharp knife.
- Attach carpet tape (available from carpet manufacturers, dealers and some supermarkets) under the edges of the damaged carpet with the adhesive side facing upwards.
- Ensure half of the tape is under the old carpet and the other half is exposed in the hole.
- Press the patch of carpet into the hole, sticking it to the exposed half of the tape.
- Brush the carpet in both directions until the fibres line up along the edge.
- Stand on the area for 5 minutes to make sure it sticks well.
- Place 10 kilos of weight – such as heavy books – on the patch for 24 hours.

GROOMING AND HEALTH

Short-haired cats are mostly self-grooming but there are times when they need a bit of hygiene help. If your cat has long hair, you'll need to groom it to prevent its hair from becoming matted. Regular grooming will also cut back on household cleaning, as there'll be less hair covering your lounge and other furniture. If your cat's hair is matting, brush it with unprocessed wheat bran. This removes excess dander (see page 56) and loosens the coat.

Because cats lick their paws when grooming, keep floors and surfaces as clean as possible. Cat paws are bacteria farms, so the cleaner a cat's environment, the cleaner its paws. If the cat's environment is dirty, wipe your cat's paws with a damp cloth once a day. Be mindful of the cleaning products used to wash floors and surfaces and avoid using harmful chemicals. Even if you believe your cat's paws are clean, they're not. The paws retain fine dirt particles that are tracked wherever the cat walks. It's why house cleaning needs to be more frequent when you have a cat.

TIP Because cats like to walk over every surface in the house, clean surfaces more regularly. Ensure cupboards are closed or your clothes and shoes could end up with poo inside them. If cats are unhappy, you'll know about it. Close washing machine lids. Cats will jump inside and often have difficulty getting out.

Cat-safe cleaning for timber floors

Timber and cork floors are usually sealed in polyurethane, tung oil, varnish or wax. For timber and cork sealed in polyurethane, clean with 1 cup of white vinegar in a 9-litre bucket of warm (not hot) water. Apply with a broom head covered in pantyhose or an old T-shirt and dry and polish as you go by standing on a towel and shuffling forward. It means you don't leave excess water on the polyurethane that can cause white bloom marks.

For timber and cork floors finished in tung oil, varnish or wax, clean with cold black tea and warm water (1 cup of tea or 3 teabags in a 9-litre bucket of water). Tea is an ideal floor cleaner because it raises the tannin levels in timber and cork, helping it retain its colour and quality. Tea also reduces the amount of dust and cat dander and the number of dust mites. Just make sure the leaves are damp, not wet. Vacuum the leaves immediately. Or tie teabags to the back of a broom and sweep. After cleaning with the tea, add a couple of drops of your favourite essential oil (Shannon uses lavender) to a bucket of water and wipe over the floor.

If the timber is unsealed, sprinkle with a little bicarb then spray over the top of it with a little white vinegar. Scrub then rinse with water.

 TIP Keep cleaning products safely stored in cupboards. Ensure caps are tightly screwed on to avoid accidental ingestion.

When you move into a new house, wipe a little butter over your cat's paws. The butter will encourage them to lick their paws, and when they walk over surfaces it will spread their scent, helping them adapt to their new home.

Cat dander

Cat dander is microscopic dead skin particles that collect in a cat's coat. The allergens in the dander can cause allergic reactions. If you have more than one cat, you'll have exponentially more dander because they groom each other. If you have a cat, clean the house once a week. For two cats, clean the house every second day. For three cats, clean every day. It's recommended that you don't own more than three cats. This is because cats are territorial and more cats equals more urine spraying.

That distinctive cat smell is caused by dander. Vacuum early and often. If you can, choose surfaces for your home that don't collect dander such as hard floors and leather couches. Minimise soft furnishings. Buy washable cat bedding – keep 2 sets. It might be tempting to use a spray to mask unpleasant cat smells but it only offers a temporary cover. The solution is to remove the dander.

 If your cat is grooming too frequently, it could be because it's nervous. If there's no obvious explanation for more frequent grooming, consult your vet.

Problem: Cat hair on upholstery
What to use: Disposable rubber gloves, cake of bathroom soap, water
How to apply: Put on a pair of disposable rubber gloves and wash your gloved hands with a cake of bathroom soap and water. Shake your hands dry. Wipe them over the upholstery. The cat hair will stick to the gloves, forming a ball that you can pluck off.

 TIP If you stroke your cat while the gloves are on, it will remove extra hair and reduce cleaning.

Washing your cat

Wear rubber gloves because cat hair is slippery when wet. Remove your cat's collar. Secure a tea towel over the cat's head and front legs, wrapping it firmly. Your cat won't be able to scratch and the darkness will be calming. Clean your cat's body with a warm, wet brush and a little cat shampoo (not regular hair shampoo – it's too alkaline for cat skin). Remove the tea towel and secure it over the cat's back legs. Wipe your cat with a damp washer from front to back. Cats love mint so apply mint tea after shampooing. If your cat is particularly grumpy, place it inside a cotton pillowcase with its head through the opening and hold the edges of the pillowcase with your hand to secure the cat. Wash it through the pillowcase. After washing, pamper your cat so it has a positive association with washing.

TIP To clean cat ears, wrap a damp cotton ball over your finger, hold it in place with your thumb and wriggle the cotton ball over your cat's ears. The cotton ball will look as though it's covered in black dust. If very dark, take the cat to the vet.

Fleas

When treating cats for fleas, it's important to interrupt the breeding cycle. Female fleas can only lay eggs if they find food within 7 to 9 days. That's why your cat will need 3 treatments every 9 days over 27 days. Flea treatments include collars, sprays, tablets, shampoos and powders. A natural solution, as long as the cat or women in the house are not pregnant, is to apply oil of pennyroyal every 2 weeks. While the cat is sleeping, put a couple of drops on your fingers and wipe between its ears and down the back of its neck to its tail. To keep flea numbers down, vacuum the house more frequently.

⚠ WARNING

Don't use oil of pennyroyal if women or cats in the house are pregnant.

Cleaning collars

Before cleaning a collar, remove the bell. If the collar is made of nylon, wet with dishwashing liquid and warm water. Then, standing over a sink, wrap the collar around a pen in a spiral pattern and hold the end with a thumb. Release your thumb and pull the other end. As the collar twists around the pencil, the dirt and water will flick off. Repeat until all the water is removed. If the collar is made of leather, rub with saddle soap and pantyhose until clean. Remove excess saddle soap by wiping over the collar with damp pantyhose. Dry in the shade so the collar doesn't go stiff. If it has metal-backed studs, dry quickly because the metal can rust.

Scratching posts

It's natural for a cat to get its claws into items, which is why a scratching post is important, particularly to save your couch. Most scratching posts are covered in a variety of surfaces including carpet, sisal and corrugated cardboard. Don't use loop pile carpet, especially nylon carpet, because it can catch cat claws. The post needs to be strong enough not to fall over when the cat leans against it. To work out where to place the post, watch where and when your cat likes to scratch. If you have the space and inclination, go crazy with a cat palace or cat tower. They can be bought or you can make your own (see page 67).

If your cat still scratches your furniture, try the following technique. As it scratches, lightly spray it with misted water. It won't like the sensation. If it still won't stop, put 1 teaspoon of naphthalene flakes or 2 mothballs in a 1-litre spray pack of water and spray in areas where it scratches, including door frames. The cat will feel as though it has Deep Heat under its claws. Reapply every 2 months.

Problem:	**Scratch marks on leather**
What to use:	**Bead of water, walnut/coloured shoe cream, cloth, stainless-steel spoon, boiling water, tea towel, leather conditioner**
How to apply:	Before tackling any stains, work out if the leather is waxed, plasticised or oiled. Place a single bead of water on an inconspicuous part of the leather. If the water soaks in slowly, it's waxed. If the water rolls off, the leather coating is plasticised. If the water soaks into the leather, it's oiled. For brown leather, cut a walnut (the nut, not the shell) in half and rub the cut surface over the area. Leave for 1 hour for the colour to cure. For other leather, use shoe cream (not shoe polish or wax) that matches the colour of the leather. Apply with a cloth over the marked area only. To set the shoe cream, rub over it with the back of a warm stainless-steel spoon (dip the spoon in a glass of boiling water and dry with a tea towel). Wipe with leather conditioner. Make your own by placing 1 teaspoon of beeswax, 1 teaspoon of lavender oil and 1 teaspoon of lemon oil on a 100 per cent cotton cloth, such as an old T-shirt. Place in the microwave in a microwave-safe dish. Microwave on high in

10-second bursts until the beeswax melts. After using the cloth, place it in a zip-lock bag and store in the freezer ready to use again.

Problem: **Scratch marks on polyurethane**
What to use: **Brasso, cloth**
How to apply: Wipe with a small amount of Brasso on a cloth using speed rather than pressure. It will look worse before it looks better.

Problem: **Scratch marks on timber**
What to use: **Tinted beeswax, cloth; or baby oil, cloth; or crayon, hair dryer, pantyhose**
How to apply: Wipe with tinted beeswax on a cloth. Alternatively, wipe with baby oil on a cloth. Alternatively, scribble with a crayon in a matching colour. Aim a hair dryer over the top to gently melt the crayon into the scratch and buff with rolled-up pantyhose.

TIP Cats like playing with the soft soil in pot plants. To stop them, cover the soil with aluminium or prickly mosses, or wipe the edges of pots with Vicks VapoRub.

TIP Don't use antiseptic cream designed for humans on your cat's wounds because it will lick the cream. Speak to your vet if wounds need treating.

Problem: Cat blood on carpet/upholstery

What to use: Cake of bathroom soap, cold water, glass, old toothbrush, cloth, paper towel; white vinegar; unprocessed wheat bran, vacuum cleaner; glycerine

How to apply: Scribble over the stain with a cake of bathroom soap dipped in water as though using a crayon. For a large area, have a glass of water with you to dip your cloth into as you go. Scrub over the stain with an old toothbrush in every direction – north, south, east and west. Remove excess soap by wiping with a cold, damp cloth. Polish the soap as though polishing a tabletop. Wipe from the centre of the stain outwards. Absorb moisture by covering the area with paper towel and standing on it. Continue to change the paper towel until it's no longer wet when you stand on it.

If you tried to remove the blood with foam upholstery cleaner or commercial spray product, neutralise first by wiping with white vinegar on a cloth. If you used liquid carpet cleaner, neutralise first by rubbing with unprocessed wheat bran and vacuuming thoroughly. When neutralised, brush with 2 drops of glycerine on a toothbrush and leave for 90 minutes. If the sofa contains horsehair or jute, it can release a tannin stain so only lightly brush across the surface.

Problem: **Cat blood on cotton/non-upholstery fabric**

What to use: **Cold water, cake of bathroom soap; glycerine, cotton ball**

How to apply: For blood on cotton or non-upholstery fabric, pour a large quantity of cold water through the stain. Scrub with a cake of bathroom soap then rub the fabric against itself using your hands. Rinse under cold water and repeat until the stain is removed. If there's a stubborn shadow mark, wipe with glycerine, leave for 90 minutes, then rub with a cake of bathroom soap. If needed, repeat again. If the stain has set, wipe with 2 drops of glycerine on a cotton ball and leave for several hours in a cool, dry place. In all cases, wash according to the fabric.

Delivering a litter

When a cat delivers a litter, it makes a big mess and is difficult to clean because of the combination of amniotic sac, blood and urea. You'll only know about it when you hear mewling. Cats generally find odd spots to deliver a litter, including under a bed or on top of a wardrobe.

If there's cat birth inside leather shoes, sprinkle with talcum powder to dry out the shoes. When dry, remove as much of the mess as possible. Wash the shoes with a cake of bathroom soap and cold water. When drying, place scrunched-up newspaper inside to keep the shape of the shoes.

On timber or pavers, mix equal parts plaster of Paris and talcum powder. For every 3 cups of mixture, add 2 tablespoons of grated soap or soap flakes. Paint the mixture 6 mm to 1.3 cm thick with a brush and allow it to dry. If it feels cold on the back of your hand, it's not dry. When dry, crack it with the back of the brush and sweep clean.

Problem:	**Cat birth on carpet**
What to use:	**Cake of bathroom soap, cold water, white vinegar, cloth, glycerine, old toothbrush**
How to apply:	If the cat delivers her litter on carpet, the carpet will need to be lifted because you'll need to clean both sides of it – you can't just clean the surface. Scribble with a cake of bathroom soap dipped in cold water, then wipe with white vinegar on a cloth. Once blood and other materials are gone, remove tannin stains by lightly brushing the surface with 2 drops of glycerine on an old toothbrush. Leave for 90 minutes. Then wipe with a damp cloth.

TIP If there's an odd smell under your house and your cat has had a litter, you'll have to go under the house to clean up. If you can't get under your house, you'll need to find someone who can. Shannon suggests contacting a plumber's apprentice because they're good at squeezing into compact areas.

Problem: **Fur ball stain on carpet**
What to use: **Glycerine, old toothbrush, cake of bathroom soap, water, cloth, paper towel**
How to apply: Fur balls often leave a red–brown stain. Treat with 2 drops of glycerine on an old toothbrush lightly wiped across the surface and leave for 24 hours. Then scribble with a cake of bathroom soap dipped in water. Wipe with a damp cloth. Absorb moisture by covering the area with paper towel and standing on it. Continue to change the paper towel until it's no longer wet when you stand on it.

DID YOU KNOW? If your cat is furiously washing behind its ears, it's a sign that rain is coming. The washing relieves ear strain caused by changing air pressure.

 Cats can be a hygiene risk for newborn babies. Never allow your cat into the baby's room, regularly wash the cat and don't place your baby on the floor where the cat has been. Keep a doormat at the door of the baby's room to wipe your feet otherwise you'll track dirt and germs into the room.

SLEEP, PLAY AND TRAVEL

Most cat bedding has removable covers that can be cleaned in the washing machine. To prevent fleas from spreading, wash covers inside a pair of pantyhose and add oil of pennyroyal or mint tea to the wash.

⚠ WARNING

*Don't use oil of pennyroyal if anyone in the house is pregnant,
including the cat.*

 To prevent neighbours' cats from coming into your garden
or yard, wipe Vicks VapoRub over a few stones or rocks
and turn them face down to prevent sun and rain damage.
Alternatively, place a mothball every 5 metres along the
top of your fence.

Cat enclosures

Because cats are carnivores and hunters, place a bell on your
cat's collar. This offers an early warning to wildlife. Cats should
be kept inside at night for a 'kitty curfew' and never allowed
into the wild because they can kill native animals such as
lizards, rodents and birds. If you don't want to keep them
inside, one option is to construct an outdoor cat enclosure in
the style of a large aviary.

If you want to see what cats get up to after dark, check
out the BBC Horizon documentary *The Secret Life of the Cat*,
which monitored the behaviour of 50 cats fitted with GPS
tagging devices. While you're sleeping, they wander into other
people's homes. It's why you might find strange cat hair in
unusual places.

 If you have a cat flap, make sure it can be locked. That way
you can keep your cat in and the neighbourhood cats out.

How to make a cat tower

A happy cat needs items to climb on such as a multi-storey tower. To make your own:

- Design and measure your tower.
- Gather materials including timber, cardboard tubes (e.g. from plastic wrap dispensers), glue, a staple gun, and fabric or carpet (non-looped, sourced from carpet manufacturers). Irregularly shaped towers are stronger.
- Using a jigsaw, cut the timber platforms. Cut a hole in each platform.
- Cut the cardboard tubes to the right length.
- Cover the timber platforms in fabric or old carpet, using glue or a staple gun.
- Place the cardboard tubes into the holes. Glue into place.
- If the tower is wobbly, secure it to an anchor point, such as the wall, so it doesn't fall over.

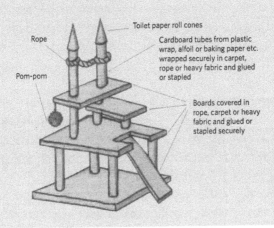

Toilet paper roll cones

Rope

Cardboard tubes from plastic wrap, alfoil or baking paper etc. wrapped securely in carpet, rope or heavy fabric and glued or stapled

Pom-pom

Boards covered in rope, carpet or heavy fabric and glued or stapled securely

How to make an outdoor cat enclosure

Cat enclosures can be bought or custom made or you can make one yourself. The construction of your 'kitty kingdom' will depend on the size and shape of your backyard. One option is to use your fence as one of the walls, with the other three sides marked out with timber. Cover the walls and roof with galvanised or plastic-coated box wire, or robust netting. Because cats love to run, attach ramps to the fence. Create an area in the enclosure where the cat can stand away from the wire, and line it with synthetic grass. Clean by rinsing or hosing with water. As long as it's diluted, urine won't affect the garden.

Cat toys

Toys keep a cat healthy, active and engaged, and it's fun to watch and play with them. As with other animals, each cat will have a favourite toy. Some like feathers, others balls of wool or items they can get their claws into. Your cat moves much faster than you do and these toys will get your moggie on the move:

- Tie cotton string to the end of a bamboo chopstick. Then tie a collection of wool or feathers to the end of the cotton string in irregular shapes. This means the chopstick will land in different ways each time. Flick the chopstick as though fly-fishing and the cat can chase it.
- Cats like tiny stuffed toys and balls. Reuse old laundry balls used in the washing machine that bounce.

- Dance a light pointer in front of their toes – never into their eyes. Don't strobe the light.
- Tie pom poms to strings attached to the back of your shoes and they'll chase you around the house.
- Cats love cardboard boxes that are the same size as they are.

Travelling with a cat

Most cats detest car travel, but sometimes the journey is necessary, such as a visit to the vet or cat kennel. The first step is to buy or hire a carrier. Ensure there's adequate food and water inside. Use their blanket and take their favourite toy. If you need to take them on a long trip, medications for motion sickness or anxiety are available from your vet.

> **Problem:** Cat urine in the car
> **What to use:** Ultraviolet light, white chalk, white vinegar, cloth, cornflour, vacuum cleaner
> **How to apply:** Inside a dark car, aim an ultraviolet light over the affected area and mark around it with white chalk so you can see where to clean. Wipe with a cloth tightly wrung out in white vinegar. Mix cornflour and white vinegar into a thick paste and place it over the car's stitching. When dry, remove and vacuum. You may need to repeat.

TIP To stop cats from sitting on your car, wipe Vicks VapoRub on the underside of the car bonnet lip.

When you are away on holiday

Cats don't like to change location. If you're heading away on a holiday or travelling interstate for work, organise for your cat to stay at a cat kennel, or ask a friend or neighbour to feed the cat. Ensure you have enough of your cat's regular food in the cupboard and ask that the kitty litter be kept clean. To give you peace of mind, ask the cat minder to send daily emails. That way, you'll know if something happens to the minder and you can call on Plan B: the back-up sitter. Leave a couple of unwashed T-shirts for your cat – the scent will be calming. Cat-sitting services often send daily pictures of your cat so you can see how well they're being cared for.

CHAPTER 3

BIRDS

The most popular pet bird in the world is the budgerigar. But according to *Bird Talk* magazine, owners voted the cockatiel their favourite pet bird because of its affectionate nature. Also high on the list is the African grey parrot, which is described as intelligent, sensitive and quiet. Because birds are sociable, it's best to have more than one. If not, ensure you have regular contact with your bird and ask it, 'Who's a pretty birdie, then?'

WHICH BIRD IS RIGHT FOR YOU?

There are big differences between breeds so do your homework first. One of the most important considerations is noise – many birds, such as parrots, often screech. What will the neighbours think? How much space do you have? The cage should be twice the size of the wingspan of the grown bird. Also be aware that some birds produce feather dust, a fine white powder, which could annoy some owners. Remember that birds have long life spans.

DID YOU KNOW? There are 41 species of native birds that can be kept as pets but they can't be trapped in the wild. If you trap them, there are hefty fines and jail terms.

FEEDING

Birds eat a varied diet. Birds such as parrots eat plants and some eat animal food, while other birds eat grains, seeds, fruits or nectar. If you're not sure what food is best for your bird, ask your vet. Add green food to their diet, such as lettuce or apple, along with cuttlefish and shell grit for beak and foot care. Cuttlefish is available at pet shops, or collect your own along the beach.

Clean seed containers in warm soapy water. Don't simply top up the container with food, because birds often leave the husks of seeds behind. Don't remove husks by blowing over them because they can easily become caught in your eyes. Instead, place the seeds into a sieve, give it a shake and the husks will fall through the sieve.

TIP Feed rainbow lorikeets outside because they make a big mess and their food is sticky and difficult to remove.

DID YOU KNOW? The question of whether to feed wild birds is a controversial one. Many Australians leave seed and food near their property to attract birds. As ecologist Professor Darryl Jones says, 'Whether you like it or not, millions of Australians feed birds. This is almost certainly changing the avian landscape, but they are not going to stop. The best we can hope for, at least until more explicit research is undertaken, is for feeders to follow some simple guidelines like keeping their feeding areas clean, avoiding bread and processed meats and not putting out too much.'[3] Experts recommend against feeding cockatoos, because if you then stop feeding them, they'll start snacking on your deck and other timber.

Problem:	**Bird poo on car**
What to use:	**Cloth, glycerine, talcum powder, pantyhose**
How to apply:	Remove the bird poo as soon as possible by wiping with a damp cloth. If the poo has hardened, leave a damp cloth over the poo for 10 minutes to soften it and then wipe clean. Remove dullness from the duco by polishing with equal parts glycerine and talcum powder on a rolled-up pair of pantyhose.

---

3   http://www.abc.net.au/radionational/programs/ockhamsrazor/seeds-of-destruction/5416254

DID YOU KNOW? In Venice, the seats on the famous gondolas used to be covered in silk until the amount of pigeon poo forced owners to change. The take-home message: pigeon poo and silk don't mix. If you're wearing silk and are unfortunately struck by poo, remove the offending poo as soon as possible. If you get bird poo in your hair, wash it straight away or the lime from the poo could spot-bleach your hair.

 TIP To deter birds, hang old CDs or DVDs from tree branches, the washing line or the back veranda. Some birds are startled by shiny reflections.

Poo on upholstery

Q: 'I let my bird out of its cage and it pooped on the couch,' reports Sandra. 'What can I do?'

Problem:	**Bird poo on couch**
What to use:	**Tissue, vacuum cleaner; cake of bathroom soap, cold water, pantyhose; dishwashing liquid; glycerine; lavender oil, cloth; leather conditioner**
How to apply:	If you see the poo drop (i.e. it's fresh), hold a tissue over the end of a vacuum cleaner hose and vacuum over the poo. It will be caught in the tissue. If the poo has dried, treat according to the bird's diet. For seed-eating birds, wipe the poo with a cake of

bathroom soap dipped in cold water on lightly dampened pantyhose. For meat-eating birds, wipe the poo with a cake of bathroom soap dipped in cold water. If the bird eats fish and insects, the poo will penetrate deeply and needs to be cleaned thoroughly because it can attract maggots; after wiping with a cake of bathroom soap dipped in cold water, rub 2 drops of dishwashing liquid into the spot and wipe with a damp cloth. For birds that eat fruit – including berries, apples and oranges – wipe the poo with glycerine, leave for 90 minutes, then wipe with a cake of bathroom soap dipped in water. If there's yellow residue, wipe with lavender oil on a cloth then wipe with a damp cloth. Clean the entire panel in even, parallel strokes or you'll get a watermark.

Bird poo can shrink leather; after cleaning a leather couch, wipe with leather conditioner. Make your own by placing 1 teaspoon of beeswax, 1 teaspoon of lavender oil and 1 teaspoon of lemon oil on a cotton cloth, such as an old T-shirt. Place in the microwave in a microwave-safe dish. Microwave on high in 10-second bursts until the beeswax melts. After using the cloth, place it in a zip-lock bag and store in the freezer ready to use again.

TIP If your bird flies freely around the house, create a branch perch area with a large sand tray underneath and your bird will poo there and not elsewhere in the house.

Problem: Bird poo on timber

What to use: Cake of bathroom soap, cold water, cloth/ pantyhose; dishwashing liquid; glycerine; lavender oil; black tea; beeswax

How to apply: For seed-eating birds, wipe poo with a cake of bathroom soap dipped in cold water on a cloth or pantyhose. For meat-eating birds, wipe poo with a cake of bathroom soap and cold water. If they eat fish and insects, the poo will penetrate deeply and needs to be cleaned thoroughly because it can attract maggots. After wiping with a cake of bathroom soap dipped in cold water, rub 2 drops of dishwashing liquid into the spot and wipe with a damp cloth. For birds that eat fruit such as berries, apples and oranges, these foods have a high tannin content so clean the poo with glycerine, leave for 90 minutes, then wipe with a cake of bathroom soap dipped in water. If there's yellow residue, wipe with lavender oil on a cloth then wipe with a damp cloth. If the timber is oiled, clean with a cake of bathroom soap dipped in cold water. You may need to clean the entire panel. After removing the stain, re-oil the timber. If there are bleach marks, wipe with strong black tea. Bird poo is very alkaline; if left on for too long, the lime in the faeces will etch a surface such as varnish and you'll need to retouch it. Polish furniture with beeswax to create a protective layer.

Problem: **Bird poo on outdoor furniture**

What to use: **Cake of bathroom soap, broom, cold water; cloth, glycerine**

How to apply: If the surface is painted, rub a cake of bathroom soap over the head of a soft, clean broom, add cold water and scrub over the poo. If the stain has set, wipe a cloth over the stain with glycerine, leave for 90 minutes, then use the above method. Avoid using detergents and, if possible, clean in the shade.

TIP Some birds can be a pest, nesting in your eaves or pooing on your veranda. To deter them, place rubber snakes in a visible area. The snakes need to be moved once a week or fortnight because the birds get used to them. Rubber snakes don't deter kookaburras; Shannon once saw a kookaburra pick one up and get a shock when it didn't wriggle.

Problem: **Bird poo on powder-coated surfaces**

What to use: **Cake of bathroom soap, cold water, cloth; or glycerine, talcum powder, pantyhose; sweet almond oil; white spirits; bicarb, white vinegar**

How to apply: Wipe with cold water and a cake of bathroom soap on a cloth. Alternatively, mix glycerine and talcum powder to form a paste, apply to the stain and leave for 1 hour. Remove with pantyhose. If it has etched the surface, wipe the entire area with sweet almond oil. If coated in rust-proof paint, use a cake of bathroom soap and cold water then wipe with white spirits on a cloth. If made of raw metal, wipe with bicarb and white vinegar. If dulled, polish the section with jeweller's rouge, a polishing compound, using a sheepskin buff on an electric drill. Some painted metal finishes will need the paint to be retouched.

Problem: **Bird poo on glass**

What to use: **Glycerine, water, spray pack, cloth; sweet almond oil**

How to apply: Mix 1 tablespoon of glycerine and 1 litre of water in a spray pack. Make sure the glass is cold, spray over the mixture and wipe with a damp cloth. If the glass looks cloudy, wipe with sweet almond oil on a cloth. Windows covered in film are more likely to be marked with poo because birds see their reflection and fly into the glass.

Problem: **Bird poo on wrought iron**

What to use: **Glycerine, white vinegar, cold water, deck scrubber/brush, cake of bathroom soap**

How to apply: Mix 1 teaspoon of glycerine, 1 teaspoon of white vinegar and 1 cup of cold water. Scrub the mixture over the stains with a deck scrubber or stiff scrubbing brush and allow to dry. Rub a cake of bathroom soap over a deck scrubber or brush, dampen with cold water and scrub over the stain. Bird poo is high in protein, so use only cold water.

Problem: **Seagull poo on canvas**

What to use: **Cake of bathroom soap, cold water, stiff brush; dishwashing liquid, cloth**

How to apply: Dip a cake of bathroom soap in cold water and scribble over the stain as though using a crayon. Scrub with a brush and rinse in cold water. If the seagulls eat fish and insects, the poo will penetrate deeply and needs to be cleaned thoroughly. After wiping with a cake of bathroom soap dipped in cold water, rub dishwashing liquid into the spot and wipe with a damp cloth.

TIP The plant varieties in your garden will attract different types of birds. Most nectar-eaters love buddleia, as do butterflies. Rainbow lorikeets love grevilleas. Native grasses and bottlebrush attract fairy wrens and silvereyes. It's a wonderful way to interact with wildlife.

GROOMING

Birds have a built-in comb: their beak. When it comes to washing, some birds like to have misted water sprayed over them while others prefer a dish of water in the base of their cage. Some prefer a full shower. Don't use sprays, oils or additives in the washing water. Budgies like to wash in a pile of lettuce leaves. Remove the leaves after washing.

Blood on carpet

Q: 'When clipping my bird's wings, I accidentally cut too close and drew blood,' says Anthony. 'The blood dripped on the carpet. How do I remove it?'

Problem:	Blood on carpet
What to use:	Cake of bathroom soap, cold water, glass, old toothbrush, cloth, paper towel; white vinegar, glycerine
How to apply:	Scribble over the stain with a cake of bathroom soap dipped in cold water. Keep a glass of water nearby. Scrub with an old toothbrush in every direction – north, south, east and west. Wipe with a cold, damp cloth. Absorb moisture by covering the area with paper towel and standing on it. Continue to replace the paper towel until it's dry. If you used another product first, neutralise by blotting with white vinegar on a cloth. Lightly brush across the carpet

with 2 drops of glycerine on an old toothbrush. Leave for 90 minutes. Then use the technique described above.

 If there's no choice but to clip a bird's wings, ask your vet to do it. It's painful when done poorly.

 Peacocks look beautiful but can be a bit noisy during springtime and mating season. Create a roosting area off the ground, such as in a tree. Their poo is great fertiliser for the garden. Keep their feathers to sell – it could cover the cost of their feed. When they first arrive at a property, they need time to adjust; hand-feeding is a good way to bond. After releasing a peacock from its pen, clip a wing so it stays in the area. Peacocks make great watchdogs.

Problem: **Bird feathers on hard floors**
What to use: **Damp broom**
How to apply: This is common, particularly during moulting. Before cleaning, close windows and doors to eliminate any breezes. Vacuuming tends to blow feathers everywhere. Instead, sweep with a clean, damp broom.

 Save bird feathers to make jewellery or to use as stuffing. To clean loose feathers, steam them. Boil a pot of water on the stove, place a cloth over the top of the pot and lay the feathers on top of the cloth. The steam will clean the feathers and won't damage them.

TIP Some birds such as parrots producer feather dust, or dander. To keep dust to a minimum, bathe birds more frequently, regularly sweep or vacuum near their cage, and change cage liners every day.

BIRD CAGES

The more spacious the cage, the happier the bird. Just make sure the bird's head can't fit between the bars, where it could get caught. The base of the cage can be lined with newspaper or paper towel that can be thrown away every day. Be aware that the paper will become soggy following contact with water. It's best not to place sandpaper at the bottom of the cage because poo, food and other gunk can become caught on it. If you have a tray of sand, when cleaning, slide the contents of the tray into a plastic bag and place in the bin straight away. You can place the contents directly into a compost bin but make sure you bury it or the old birdseed will germinate. If you want to germinate the seed, cut an edge off a large potato and hollow it out. Put a small amount of cotton wool inside and place the seed on top of the cotton wool. When the seed grows, the potato will resemble a 'potato porcupine' that your bird will love pecking.

Birds love to bathe. It keeps them healthy. Ensure your birdbath is large enough and has a spill cloth underneath, or use a baby feeding tray with a rim that can't be knocked over.

You can buy perches made of plastic, stone or wood, or make your own from a eucalyptus twig. Eucalyptus is ideal for beak and claw cleaning and your bird will be healthier from the eucalyptus and other volatile oils in the branch. Avoid perches made of sandpaper because it can cause lesions on your bird's feet.

Cleaning bird cages

In the wild, birds drop their poo and fly away – they don't sleep near their faeces. Bird poo can cause corrosion on the wires of a birdcage and muck inside the cage because it can cause sickness. Clean the cage once a week. Remove seed and water containers and place the entire cage in the kitchen sink. Run water over the cage, gently giving your bird a bath at the same time. Help distribute the water in a spray by aiming it at the cage wire. Alternatively, place the cage in the shower with enough space for the bird to step out of the flow of water. Leave the cage to drain and air-dry inside or outside the house. A third option is to clean the cage outside over a garden bed. The poop makes great fertiliser. The birdseed will grow as a weed and it's easy to pull out because it's a single-root plant. Collect the seed heads to feed to your bird.

Commercial bird poo removers are available but Shannon prefers to clean cages with a cake of bathroom soap and cold water on a cloth, before wiping with white vinegar on a cloth. To protect the wire from further corrosion, wipe with sweet almond oil or vegetable oil on a cloth.

Problem: **Algae in birdbath**
What to use: **Pantyhose, non-iodised salt**
How to apply: Remove water from the birdbath and wipe over the algae with a rolled-up pair of

pantyhose. To prevent the problem from returning, add a pinch of non-iodised salt to each litre of clean water. The birds won't be deterred by the tiny amount of salt, but the algae will.

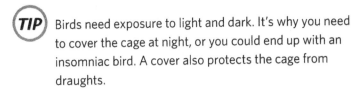 Birds need exposure to light and dark. It's why you need to cover the cage at night, or you could end up with an insomniac bird. A cover also protects the cage from draughts.

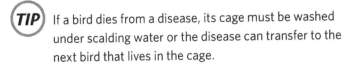 If a bird dies from a disease, its cage must be washed under scalding water or the disease can transfer to the next bird that lives in the cage.

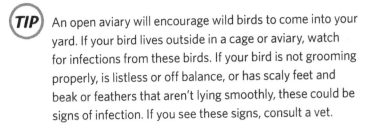 An open aviary will encourage wild birds to come into your yard. If your bird lives outside in a cage or aviary, watch for infections from these birds. If your bird is not grooming properly, is listless or off balance, or has scaly feet and beak or feathers that aren't lying smoothly, these could be signs of infection. If you see these signs, consult a vet.

CHICKENS

A steady supply of free-range eggs is just one of the benefits of keeping hens. There are many varieties, with popular pet choices including Australorps, Leghorns and Isabrowns. If you're unsure about becoming a full-time chook owner, you can rent one and see how you go. Most urban councils allow you to keep hens, but rules differ on roosters because of their early-morning crowing. Some councils allow you to have a rooster as long as it's kept in a night box. The coop must be clean and the chickens healthy. Most owners clip their birds' wings to make sure the chooks don't accidentally escape the yard.

Feeding

Most chickens eat a combination of poultry pellets and kitchen scraps. Avoid feeding them meat and fats. According to the RSPCA, you shouldn't feed chickens avocado, rhubarb, citrus fruits, onion, garlic, chocolate or lawn mower clippings (the clippings can become mouldy). Ensure the feed container is rodent-proof. Chickens love to eat weeds so let them go free-range. Access to fresh water is important.

TIP Chook poo is a great fertiliser and rots quickly because of the high lime content.

Q: 'I sat on the couch not realising there was chicken poo on my pants,' reports Anne. 'How can I remove it?

Problem:	**Chicken poo on upholstery and carpet**
What to use:	**Paper towel, white vinegar, cloth, cake of bathroom soap, cold water**
How to apply:	Remove quickly because lime can bleach fabric or carpet. Absorb excess with paper towel. Remove lime by wiping with a cloth

tightly wrung out in white vinegar. Then remove protein by scribbling with a cake of bathroom soap dipped in cold water. Wipe with a damp cloth. If the upholstery or carpet is bleached, re-dye it (see page 99).

Problem:	**Chicken urine on carpet**
What to use:	**Paper towel, white vinegar, cloth**
How to apply:	Remove quickly because lime can bleach the carpet. Absorb excess with paper towel. Place white vinegar on a cloth and wring tightly so it's damp but not wet. Rub from the outside to the inside of the stain. Absorb moisture by covering the area with paper towel and standing on it. Continue to change the paper towel until it's no longer wet when you stand on it.

Chicken coops

Your coop must be able to be locked at night to protect your chooks from foxes and other predators. Clean it each week and add fresh straw to the base. Chickens need to roam outside their coop for at least 1 hour a day.

DID YOU KNOW? At the 2015 Global Pet Expo, the Most Outrageous New Pet Products included a harness for pet chickens so owners could take them for a walk.

DUCKS

If you have a snail, slug or weed problem, the solution could be pet ducks. It's recommended you have more than one because they are social animals. Ducks must be kept in a cage made from solid sheeting or welded mesh – chicken wire isn't strong enough. And because they product a lot of poo, their cage needs to be cleaned 3 times a week. Water supply is very important.

Problem: **Duck poo on carpet**

What to use: **Talcum powder, plastic comb, cake of bathroom soap, cold water, pantyhose, paper towel**

How to apply: Duck poo is very slimy. Sprinkle it with talcum powder to absorb moisture. Remove as much poo as possible by lifting with a plastic comb. Scribble with a cake of bathroom soap dipped in cold water as though using a crayon. Rub with damp rolled-up pantyhose in all directions – north, south, east and west. Absorb moisture by covering the area with paper towel and standing on it. Continue to change the paper towel until it's no longer wet when you stand on it.

 TIP Ducks moult in late summer/early autumn lose all their feathers. Drakes also go through a partial moult in early summer. Because duck feathers and waterbird feathers are waterproof, they have value. Collect them to sell.

CHAPTER 4

FISH

When mega-successful movie *Finding Nemo* was first released, sales of clownfish soared. But with only half of the clownfish stock bred in captivity, and the other half taken from reefs, it led to a shocking decline in the wild population of these famous fish. It's a reminder to buy pet fish from reputable breeders. In Australia, more than 20.5 million fish are kept as pets. Owners enjoy the calm and colour they bring to a home. One reason for their growing popularity is the rise in apartment living; fish make for low-maintenance and quiet pets. Just remember that tank cleaning is an essential part of keeping a pet fish.

WHICH FISH IS RIGHT FOR YOU?

The first step is to research the type of fish you'd like: freshwater or tropical. This influences the habitat required to keep them. Freshwater fish need specific water chemistry whereas tropical fish need specific water temperature. When choosing fish, look at the scale pattern and avoid fish with raised scales, discolouring or white patches. Eyes should be clear, not milky. The stomach shouldn't be distended. The fish should be able to swim to the bottom of the tank.

FEEDING

Feed fish according to their breed. Tropical fish eat differently from freshwater fish. Feed at the same time each day – morning and evening – preferably in the same spot in the tank. Only feed an amount of food that can be eaten in 5 minutes. If food remains after 5 minutes, remove it from the tank – goldfish can die from overeating. If tank decorations are covered in algae, it could indicate you're using too much feed. Fish like variety in their diet, so mix it up.

DID YOU KNOW? Fish are the most popular pet in the United States, with more pet fish than cats and dogs combined.

FISH TANKS

Choose the most appropriately sized tank and filter for your breed of fish. Because fish produce ammonia, which is poisonous in large quantities, ensure that the tank is a good size, with an appropriate water filter. You'll need a tank with a lid and light, gravel, ornaments, food, water-conditioning fluid, siphon, hose and bucket. If placed on a stand, make sure it is stable. Build the contents of your tank around the needs of the fish. For example, because goldfish are prey animals, there should be plants and ornaments for the goldfish to hide in or they'll feel stressed. To reduce algal outbreaks, place tanks away from direct sunlight and windows, and avoid putting them in high-traffic areas such as hallways.

Be careful when adding new water to an existing fish tank because sudden changes in temperature can kill fish. If the water level has dropped and you need to add more, fill a plastic bag with fresh water, sit the bag in the existing tank water until the water inside the plastic bag is the same temperature as the water in the tank, then slowly add the new water to the tank water.

Cleaning fish tanks – weekly

According to University of Western Australia science researcher Miriam Sullivan, 'Fish are the forgotten family pet. Just like cats and dogs, fish are intelligent, long-lived and can feel pain, but you would never flush your dead cat down a toilet or win puppies at carnivals. With 1.5 billion pet fish sold globally every year, it's time we started taking better care of them and regularly cleaning out an aquarium is one of the most effective ways to keep your fish healthy.'[4]

---

4   theconversation.com/the-goldfish-test-that-can-change-your-behaviour-22672

An average fish tanks holds 40 litres or over. Clean weekly. There's no need to remove the fish or the contents of the tank.

- If there's algae, wipe the inside of the glass with pantyhose pulled over your hand like a mitt. Do this before removing any water.
- Remove 15 per cent of the water.
- Clean 25 per cent of the gravel with a siphon. Or remove 25 per cent of the gravel, place it in a sieve and flush with boiling water. Allow to dry.
- If you need to clean the filter, don't change all the water at the same time. Rinse a new filter under cold running water.
- To clean algae from decorations, place them inside a plastic bag with sand, close the bag tightly and shake clean.
- Replace the water (match water temperature – see page 169). If it's a large amount of water, transfer it from a bucket (uncontaminated with detergents) using a siphon. Leave a gap between the top of the water and the top of the tank for oxygen exchange.
- Wipe the outside of the tank with white vinegar on a cloth. Never use strong detergents because they can seep into the water and harm your fish.

Small fish tanks (under 40 litres) need to be cleaned twice a week with 50 per cent water change. If your tank doesn't have a filter, water should be changed every day – between 50 to 100 per cent.

Cleaning large tanks with fish inside

Use a piece of glass that's the same width as the fish tank. Remove rocks and plants from the tank. Place the piece of glass inside the tank at one end and gradually move it along the tank until it reaches the middle of the tank. The fish will be on one side of the glass. Clean the non-fish area of the tank with a gravel cleaner. Let the water settle then repeat the process on the other side of the tank. It means the fish don't have to be removed from the tank and adjust to new water. If there is significant algae, when you rub along the side the water will be filthy until the filter cleans it. As you clean, place a submersible filter unit inside the tank – if the solid matter is too high, the fish won't be able to breathe.

Cleaning fish tanks – quarterly

- During a comprehensive clean of a large tank, unplug the heater.
- Remove plants and decorations and wipe over the inside of the glass with pantyhose – wrap the pantyhose over your hand to create a mitt.
- Using a fish net, transfer fish to a large glass bowl that's been rinsed with hot water. Add water scooped from the fish tank to lessen the shock to the fish. Put 1 or 2 plants or decorations from the tank into the bowl. Don't leave the fish there for more than 30 minutes.
- Siphon at least 25 per cent and no more than 50 per cent of the tank water into a bucket designated for the task so there's no contamination from detergent residue. Never use

soap, detergents or old kitchen sponges when cleaning a fish tank because they're harmful to fish.

- Remove the filter and clean it in the sink.
- Use a gravel cleaner to clean gravel, or place in a sieve and flush with boiling water. Allow to dry.
- Match the temperature of the water for replacement and refill the tank.
- Replace plants and ornaments and reconnect the filter.
- Add salt or conditioner.
- Plug in the heater and restart the pump. Leave for 15 minutes before returning the fish.
- Wipe the outside of the tank with white vinegar on a cloth. Never use strong detergents because they can seep into the water and harm your fish.

 Choose live plants for your fish tank over plastic ones. They oxygenate the water.

 Algae is great fertiliser for the garden. Wipe along the glass with a rolled-up pair of pantyhose, then rinse in water and toss the water on the garden.

Filters

Filtration can be mechanical, biological or chemical and several styles of filter are available. Clean according to the instructions. If there's an outbreak of algae, the filter may need flushing or replacing. Also ensure that the filter is big enough for the tank.

To clean pebbles, reach inside the tank with a pair of pantyhose and place the pebbles inside one leg. Lift the pebble-filled pantyhose out of the tank over a bowl and transfer to the sink. Flush the pebbles inside the pantyhose backwards and forwards under hot water until clean.

Tropical fish need a water temperature of between 24 and 27 degrees Celsius, with some requiring warmer and others cooler temperatures. Check the temperature with a thermometer – one that sticks on the side of the aquarium is easiest. Many have visual indicators that let you know if the water is too hot or too cold.

Constant heat and moisture can cause mould in high-humidity areas. To remove mould on the outside of the tank, mix ¼ teaspoon of oil of cloves in a 1-litre spray pack of water. Don't spray oil of cloves directly onto the tank. Instead, spray the mixture onto a cloth and wipe over the affected area. Oil of cloves is a sedative and can kill fish.

Most aerosols affect fish, so be careful using air fresheners, insecticide sprays and perfumes. The owners of Snowy, a goldfish, learnt this the hard way when they released a cockroach bomb in their apartment before going on holiday. When a friend came over to feed Snowy, there was bad news. Snowy didn't survive the bomb. Avoid using air freshener dispensers or plug-in deodorisers that are harmful to fish; they also cause stains on walls, floors and furniture.

You can reduce the amount of cleaning needed in an aquarium by adding suckerfish, sometimes called 'vacuum-cleaner fish', to the tank. Options include catfish, nerite snails, cory catfish, plecostomus catfish, loaches, Chinese algae eaters, crayfish and tiger shovel-nosed catfish. Don't add too many, because if they run out of food, they'll attack the fish. If the tank is too clean, you've got too many suckerfish. Another way to reduce cleaning is to use a water garden tank that has plants on top of it. These remove toxins.

Fish tank maintenance

Each day, check pumps, filters and water temperature. Each week, check electrical connections to the tank. If the filter is located under gravel, replace carbon or polyfibre wool or mesh once a week or according to the instructions. For other systems, replace every 5 weeks. If the tank sits on a stand, check the stand regularly for cracks or damage.

As with any standing water, mozzies will lay their eggs in it, so keep a cover over the tank. Remove the cover for a couple of minutes each day to oxygenate the water – while feeding is ideal. Never use mozzie spray over the top of the tank because you'll kill the fish.

If there are heavy water stains on the glass, the news isn't good. It isn't lime deposit, but glass cancer from not changing the water frequently enough. Water conditioners can leave a tidemark on the glass that can't be fixed. Ensure the water level remains above the line of the affected glass. Regularly change the water.

How to repair cracks in fish tank glass

During repair, remove the fish and other items and drain the tank of water. Wipe over the area to be repaired with white vinegar on a cloth. Remove white vinegar residue by wiping with a cloth wrung in boiling water. Fill the crack with glass glue or glass adhesive that sets when exposed to UV light. It's available from hardware stores. Ensure the crack has no bubble lines. Remove the excess. Then set the glue by placing the glass in the sun for 2 minutes. It won't set unless exposed to sunlight.

 TIP Never release goldfish into the wild. It's bad news for the goldfish and bad news for native animals, particularly native frogs that keep insect larvae under control. If your goldfish dies, bury it in the garden under a citrus tree, rose bush or geranium. Don't flush it down the toilet – think of Nemo. If you have fish in outdoor ponds and there's a flood, make sure the fish don't leave your property.

Q: 'My 3-year-old, Harley, took it upon himself to clean the fish tank,' reports John. 'He woke early, grabbed a bucket and filled it with water, carting it from the bathroom to the lounge room and back. As a consequence, the carpet is sodden with water. Help!'

Problem: Carpet flooded with water

What to use: Steam cleaner, cleaning chemicals, bicarb, white vinegar, methylated spirits, glycerine, eucalyptus oil, hot water

How to apply: Steam cleaners are available for hire at the supermarket and come with a bottle of carpet cleaning chemicals. Run the steam cleaner on empty to remove excess moisture. Then add half the amount of carpet cleaning chemicals and top them up with 2 tablespoons of bicarb, 2 tablespoons of white vinegar, 2 tablespoons of methylated spirits, 2 teaspoons of glycerine and 2 teaspoons of eucalyptus oil. Fill with hot water and steam the carpet. Run the steam cleaner on empty until the moisture is drawn out.

DIY carpet dye

If you don't remove the water in time and the carpet is ruined, you can re-dye it. Not all carpets can be re-dyed but you're in luck if you have wool or nylon carpet. Also be aware that carpet can only be re-dyed in a colour that's darker than the original. Dark brown, blue or purple are the most popular re-dye colours. Clear the room of furniture and use a steam cleaner over the carpet. When completely dry, apply the dye according to the instructions. Do a test patch first. A steam cleaner is generally the best way to apply dye.

Outdoor fish ponds

If you keep fish in an outside pond, place a net over the water
or add water lilies so the fish can hide from birds. Water lilies
will clean the water and the floating root system will act as a
filter, keeping the water oxygenated. Good pond plants include
Bacopa caroliana and eel grass. Make sure you avoid water
hyacinth, which is described as the world's worst aquatic weed
because it can cover entire waterways. Use native plants, not
introduced ones.

CHAPTER 5

HORSES

On the first Tuesday in November, the nation stops for a horse race. We're still enamoured of champion horse Phar Lap. Many words and phrases in our language are equine-related, such as 'workhorse' to describe a dependable performer, and 'horseplay'. And while modern living means we have less contact with horses, they are still popular pets. There are strict guidelines on keeping horses in urban areas – consult your local council or pound for regulations. Before deciding to keep a horse as a pet, spend time at a local stable to get first-hand experience of what's involved.

FEEDING

Horses are herbivores and eat grass and plants. Pasture-fed is best, and this can be supplemented with hay if needed.

 Horses love to eat watermelon rind, crunchy fruits and vegetables such as pumpkin, carrots and cucumbers.

Make your own trough

Make your own trough from an old bathtub. Cast-iron and polycarbonate baths are ideal because these materials are sturdy and won't easily break. Look for discarded baths at council clean-ups or at the tip. Once you position the tub, add hosing or conduit pipe under the sinkhole to allow for drainage and put a deep bathplug in the hole. Surround the edges of the bath with soil, with the edges steep enough for the horse to stand in front of but not inside the tub to prevent water fouling. Place sod over the top of the soil to help keep the water cool and position rocks around the edges of the trough. It will resemble a little lake in a hilltop.

The trough water will develop algae and is an ideal breeding ground for mozzies. Don't simply top up the water but empty the entire tub before refilling with fresh water. The frequency with which you change the water will depend on the weather. During winter, you'll only need to change the water once a week. During summer, it could be every second day. Change the water whenever you see algae.

Horses need plenty of water. The average horse drinks 30 to 50 litres of water per day – more during hot weather. Your horse will need less water if eating green feed.

TIP To remove urine stains from your horse, wipe with white vinegar on a clean towel. For a dry bath, mix unprocessed wheat bran and white vinegar and brush through its coat. For oily marks, place a couple of drops of dishwashing liquid on your fingers and massage into the stain until it feels like jelly. Then wipe with a damp cloth.

Problem: **Horse urine on clothing**
What to use: **White vinegar, cloth**
How to apply: Wipe over the urine with white vinegar on a cloth. Then wash normally.

Problem: **Horse manure on clothing**
What to use: **Cake of bathroom soap, cold water; or white spirits, cloth**
How to apply: If fresh, wipe with a cake of bathroom soap and cold water. Then wash normally. If old, wipe with white spirits on a cloth. Leave for 5 minutes. Then wash normally.

Problem: **Horse manure on leather boots**
What to use: **Sunshine, shoe brush; cheap shampoo, blood-heat (body temperature) water, cloth, newspaper; leather conditioner**
How to apply: Place the boots in sunshine and allow the manure to dry out. Use a shoe brush to remove as much manure as you can from the boots. If the manure has penetrated through the

leather, wipe with cheap shampoo and blood-heat (body temperature) water on a cloth then flush with blood-heat water. Dry slowly in the shade with newspaper inside the boots to hold their shape. In all cases, wipe with leather conditioner on a cloth to give a protective surface. Make your own by placing 1 teaspoon of beeswax, 1 teaspoon of lavender oil and 1 teaspoon of lemon oil on a 100 per cent cotton cloth, such as an old T-shirt. Place in the microwave in a microwave-safe dish. Microwave on high in 10-second bursts until the beeswax melts. After using the cloth, place it in a zip-lock bag and store in the freezer ready to use again.

Manure on stable walls

Q: 'How do you get old manure stains off the walls of the stable?' asks Jack.

Problem:	**Horse manure on timber**
What to use:	**Sunshine/hair dryer, stiff brush, cake of bathroom soap, cold water; plaster of Paris, glycerine**
How to apply:	Dry the timber in sunshine or with a hair dryer. Remove as much manure as possible. Coat the bristles of a stiff brush with a cake of bathroom soap and cold water and scrub over

the stain. Allow to dry. If stains remain, mix plaster of Paris and water to the consistency of peanut butter. Add 1 teaspoon of glycerine per cup of mixture and paint over the stain with a brush. Allow to dry completely. If it feels cold on the back of your hand, it's not dry. When dry, crack it with the back of the brush and sweep away. Plaster dust can be harmful to horses, so ensure it's completely removed.

 TIP Horse slobber attracts insects. Remove saliva by wiping with a damp cloth.

GROOMING AND TACK

Horses need to be groomed every day, especially if housed in a stall. Grooming is less important if the horse is in a paddock because it can rub against rocks and trees. Regularly check your horse's coat for parasites, bites and scratches. Remove sweat by rinsing with water. If very dirty, wash with horse shampoo or a small amount of dishwashing liquid, which is milder than horse shampoo. It's common to only wash the tail and mane. The wash frequency will depend on the time of year, activity level of your horse and oiliness of the coat. To make your horse's coat shine and prevent matting, place a small amount of glycerine on its brush during grooming.

The pests that bother humans also bother horses. If your horse attracts an excessive number of flies, consult your vet.

To inhibit nasties, mix 1 litre of water, 4 teaspoons of dried mint and 5 heads of lavender or 1 teaspoon of lavender oil in a saucepan. Bring to the boil, let the mixture stand for 15 minutes then place in spray pack. When cold, spray the mixture over the horse's coat and brush with a damp brush. It cleans their coat and deters bugs.

DID YOU KNOW? Because horsehair is very strong and supple, it was traditionally used to make rope, twine and plumber's insulation, and to stuff mattresses and chairs. Even today, it's used to make wigs and jewellery.

Cleaning saddles

Clean leather saddles by rolling a pair of pantyhose into a ball to the size of a mandarin. Dampen it with water and wipe over the saddle. Then apply saddle soap with the pantyhose and rub it over the leather. When there's no drag on the leather, remove excess saddle soap with paper towel or a dry, clean cloth. To prevent colour transfer to clothing, seal the leather by wiping with leather conditioner on a cloth. Make your own by placing 1 teaspoon of beeswax, 1 teaspoon of lavender oil and 1 teaspoon of lemon oil on a 100 per cent cotton cloth, such as an old T-shirt. Place in the microwave in a microwave-safe dish. Microwave on high in 10-second bursts until the beeswax melts. After using the cloth, place it in a zip-lock bag and store in the freezer ready to use again. To clean synthetic saddles, rinse with dishwashing liquid and cold water. Dry cleaned saddles thoroughly.

Cleaning riding gear and harnesses

Riding gear and harnesses often have metal buckles. To clean metal, place a small amount of white vinegar on pantyhose then add bicarb. While it's fizzing, wipe over the metal. Then wipe with a damp cloth. To prevent rust, after cleaning, wipe with a small amount of beeswax or leather conditioner. Make your own by placing 1 teaspoon of beeswax, 1 teaspoon of lavender oil and 1 teaspoon of lemon oil on a 100 per cent cotton cloth, such as an old T-shirt. Place in the microwave in a microwave-safe dish. Microwave on high in 10-second bursts until the beeswax melts. After using the cloth, place it in a zip-lock bag and store in the freezer ready to use again.

Cleaning saddle pads

If you don't clean your horse's saddle pad, horsehairs can prickle the horse's back. To remove horsehair from the saddle pad, put on a pair of disposable rubber gloves, wash your gloved hands with a cake of bathroom soap and water and rub over the saddle pad. The horsehair will stick to the gloves. Wash the saddle pad according to the washing instructions. If made of wool, wash in 1 teaspoon of cheap shampoo and blood-heat (body temperature) water. Rinse in 1 teaspoon of cheap hair conditioner and blood-heat water. Gently wring and dry flat on a towel in the shade. Don't use woolwash.

To clean canvas, mix 1 kilo of non-iodised salt in a 9-litre bucket of water. Hang the canvas over a fence and sweep thoroughly with the salt water solution. Allow to dry. When a salt crust forms, brush the salt off with a broom. Don't be surprised if the horse licks the canvas – horses love salt.

Cleaning copper

Q: 'I have horse bits made with copper,' says Mark. 'How can I clean them?'

Problem:	**Tarnished copper**
What to use:	**Bicarb, pantyhose, white vinegar, sweet almond oil**
How to apply:	Sprinkle bicarb over a pair of pantyhose and add white vinegar. While it's fizzing, wipe over the copper. When clean, prevent tarnish by wiping with sweet almond oil.

Problem:	**Tarnished brass**
What to use:	**Bicarb, pantyhose, white vinegar, sweet almond oil**
How to apply:	It's common to use brass in stables. Sprinkle bicarb over a pair of pantyhose and add white vinegar. While it's fizzing, wipe over the brass. When clean, prevent tarnish by wiping with sweet almond oil.

TIP Horses can become sunburnt. If yours has white skin under its hair, protect it with a cover, sunblock and shade.

Cleaning rubber

To clean rubber, scrub with non-iodised salt and wipe clean. To prevent perishing, mix equal parts talcum powder and glycerine and wipe over the rubber. This slows the perishing process.

Problem: Soiled satin

What to use: Talcum powder, hair dryer, cloth, cheap hair shampoo, cold water, towels

How to apply: Remove solid matter by sprinkling with talcum powder and drying with a hair dryer. Wipe with a cloth in the direction of the grain. Hand wash in 1 teaspoon of cheap hair shampoo and 9 litres of cold water. Soak for 5 minutes and rinse thoroughly under cold water. Don't wring satin. Instead, to remove water, place the item on a clean towel and roll the towel, applying pressure as you roll. To dry, lay the item flat in the shade on a clean towel. Iron on a medium heat.

Problem: Grass on clothing

What to use: Cold water, white spirits, cloth

How to apply: Remove excess grass under the tap using cold water. Wipe with white spirits on a cloth. Wash according to the fabric.

Cleaning halters and leads

To clean nylon halters and leads, add 1 teaspoon of dishwashing liquid to a 9-litre bucket of blood-heat (body temperature) water. Immerse the halter or lead. Standing over a sink, wrap the item around a pen in a spiral pattern and hold the end with a thumb. Release your thumb and pull the other end. As the lead or halter twists around the pencil, the dirt and water will flick off. Repeat until all the water is removed.

To clean leather halters and leads, rub with saddle soap on pantyhose until clean. Remove excess saddle soap by wiping with damp pantyhose. Dry in the shade so the item doesn't go stiff. If there's brass on the leather, protect the brass while cleaning by covering it with plastic wrap. To clean brass, sprinkle bicarb over pantyhose and then add white vinegar. While it fizzes, wipe over the brass. When clean, wipe brass and leather with leather conditioner. Make your own by placing 1 teaspoon of beeswax, 1 teaspoon of lavender oil and 1 teaspoon of lemon oil on a 100 per cent cotton cloth, such as an old T-shirt. Place in the microwave in a microwave-safe dish. Microwave on high in 10-second bursts until the beeswax melts. After using the cloth, place it in a zip-lock bag and store in the freezer ready to use again.

Problem:	**Dirt on clothing**
What to use:	**Cold water, Vanish NapiSan Oxi Action, blood-heat to hot water, spatula, bicarb, white vinegar**
How to apply:	Remove excess dirt under the tap with cold water. Mix Vanish NapiSan Oxi Action and blood-heat (body temperature) to hot water to the consistency of spreadable butter and place

over the stain with your fingers or a spatula. Leave for 5 minutes and wash in the washing machine according to the fabric. Don't use on wool, silk or leather. To remove red dirt, wash clothing in the washing machine with 2 tablespoons of bicarb in the washing water and 2 tablespoons of white vinegar in the fabric conditioner slot of the machine. Add ¼ of the recommended quantity of washing powder for a top loading machine and ⅛ of the recommended washing powder for a front-loading machine.

Problem:	**Leather dye marks on clothing**
What to use:	**Methylated spirits, cloth; SOS Colour Run, water; leather conditioner**
How to apply:	It's common to get marks on clothing from leather dye in new saddles, particularly if the saddle isn't coated in beeswax. To remove stains, wipe with methylated spirits on a cloth. If there's still staining, mix 1 part SOS Colour Run remover to 5 parts water and wipe over fabric on a cloth until the dye stain moves. To prevent colour transfer, wipe saddle with leather conditioner. Make your own by placing 1 teaspoon of beeswax, 1 teaspoon of lavender oil and 1 teaspoon of lemon oil on a 100 per cent cotton cloth, such as an old T-shirt. Place in the microwave in

a microwave-safe dish. Microwave on high in 10-second bursts until the beeswax melts. After using the cloth, place it in a zip-lock bag and store in the freezer ready to use again.

Cleaning footwear used around horses

To keep rubber boots looking glossy, mix equal parts glycerine and sweet almond oil and wipe with a cloth. To remove nasty smells inside rubber shoes, mix 2 tablespoons of bicarb, 2 tablespoons of talcum powder, 2 drops of tea tree oil, 2 drops of oil of cloves and 2 drops of lavender oil. Add 2 tablespoons of unprocessed wheat bran and 1 teaspoon of salt. Place the mixture in the centre of a small piece of muslin or cotton voile and tie with string or ribbon. Alternatively, place inside a pair of pantyhose and tie up. Rub through the shoe. Hang on to the ball to use again.

Because there's always moisture around horses, regularly clean leather shoes with boot polish or leather conditioner. Make your own by placing 1 teaspoon of beeswax, 1 teaspoon of lavender oil and 1 teaspoon of lemon oil on a 100 per cent cotton cloth, such as an old T-shirt. Place in the microwave in a microwave-safe dish. Microwave on high in 10-second bursts until the beeswax melts. After using the cloth, place it in a zip-lock bag and store in the freezer ready to use again.

SLEEP AND TRAVEL

Stables should be cleaned each day or you'll end up with a horrible smell and possible health problems for your horse. When cleaning, remove the horse, feed tubs and other loose items from the stable. If the stall is covered with straw, sift through it with a pitchfork – the straw that falls through isn't fouled and can be reused. Sweep the clean straw to the side of the stable. Remove the fouled straw in a wheelbarrow or 'muck bucket' and take it to the manure pile. If the stable has a soil base, allow the base to air before adding new straw. If the stable has concrete flooring, lift the straw and sweep the concrete with a wet broom before adding fresh straw. Replace the straw to a height that reaches halfway up the horse's hocks. It acts as a mattress for your horse's feet and absorbs urine and poo. Return the feed tubs and other items. Ensure the horse's hooves are clean or they can become infected.

Most stables place manure in a compost bin to sell as fertiliser. Smaller stables mix fouled straw and manure, allow it to rot, bag it and offer it for free on the side of the road. Horse manure is a particularly effective fertiliser for roses.

If there's mould (not moss or algae) in the stable, mix ¼ teaspoon of oil of cloves in a 1-litre spray pack of water. Spray onto a broom head and brush over the mould. Leave for 24 hours and repeat.

 TIP Horses don't like standing in the one place all day.

Travelling with horses

The main concerns for horses travelling long distances are respiratory problems and dehydration. Stop every 4 hours and allow the horse to put its head down to eat hay and drain fluids. Horses can be fussy about their water and don't like drinking water from different areas. One suggestion is to disguise water by adding molasses, apple juice or cordial to it. Stay at racecourses, showgrounds or pony club grounds. Plan before you leave.

CHAPTER 6

OTHER PETS

According to a *Pet Ownership in Australia* report, 'other animals' account for 2.2 million pets in Australia and include reptiles and small mammals such as rabbits and guinea pigs.[5] One reason for the growing popularity of alternative pets is urbanisation, with more people living in apartments that have restrictions on the type of pets that can be kept. These pets are often easier and cheaper to look after and generally make less noise. Thoroughly research the behaviour and needs of a pet before bringing it home.

5   http://animalmedicinesaustralia.org.au/wp-content/uploads/2015/06/
    AMA-Pet-Ownership-in-Australia-5-AUGUST-2013.pdf

RABBITS

Elmer Fudd was never able to catch that 'wascally wabbit' Bugs Bunny. Unlike the cartoon creation, rabbits are not devious creatures but very social animals that can live indoors or outdoors.

Feeding

Rabbits are herbivores and eat hay and green leafy vegetables. It means their poo is like a pellet and easy to clean. Wearing disposable rubber gloves, simply pick it up, place it in a plastic bag and dispose of it – it doesn't stain, except in the unfortunate circumstance of diarrhoea. Don't place rabbit poo directly on the garden because it's acidic and will kill plants. But it's an ideal weed killer. Allow the poo to rot for around 6 weeks and place over weeds.

Another piece of good news is that a rabbit will keep lawn mowing to a minimum because it nibbles at weeds and grass, and will happily chomp on lawn daisy, oxalis, dandelion and plumbago. Clean feeding bowls in the sink with dishwashing liquid and hot water. Rinse with clean water and dry thoroughly.

Rabbit teeth continue to grow throughout their life and chewing helps to keep their teeth chiselled.

Problem: Rabbit diarrhoea on carpet/upholstery
What to use: Plastic comb, paper towel, talcum powder, cake of bathroom soap, cold water, pantyhose; dishwashing liquid, cloth

How to apply: Remove excess by lifting the solids with a plastic comb or by blotting liquids with paper towel. Create an edge around the stain with either talcum powder or paper towel. Work from the outside to the inside of the stain. Scribble over the stained area with a cake of bathroom soap dipped in cold water as though using a crayon. Wipe with damp pantyhose rolled in a ball. If any stain remains, massage with 2 drops of dishwashing liquid on your fingertips until the liquid feels like jelly. Wipe with a damp cloth until the dishwashing liquid is removed. Absorb moisture by covering the area with paper towel and standing on it. Continue to change the paper towel until it's no longer wet when you stand on it.

Problem: **Rabbit diarrhoea on non-upholstery fabric**

What to use: **Cake of bathroom soap, cold water; or Vanish NapiSan Oxi Action, bucket, cold water; sunshine**

How to apply: Scribble with a cake of bathroom soap dipped in cold water as though using a crayon. Alternatively, mix ½ lid of Vanish NapiSan Oxi Action in a 9-litre bucket of cold water and soak for 20 minutes. (Don't use Vanish NapiSan Oxi Action on silk or wool.) Wash according to the fabric. Dry in sunshine.

Rabbits are very heat-sensitive. On hot days, wrap frozen water bottles or frozen ice blocks in damp towels or sterilisation wrap and place inside the hutch. If there are 2 or more frozen blocks, a rabbit can wedge between them.

Problem: Dirty litter box
What to use: White vinegar, water
How to apply: Remove the contents of the litter box and rinse with water. Add 5 mm of white vinegar to the base of the box. Leave for 20 minutes, then rinse with water and dry.

Old urine on carpet

Q: 'I'm having difficulty removing dried rabbit urine from the carpet,' says Mick. 'Any suggestions?'

Problem: Old rabbit urine on carpet
What to use: Glycerine, old toothbrush, cloth, white vinegar; ultraviolet light, white chalk; paper towel
How to apply: If the urine has penetrated to the back of the carpet, the jute will release a tannin stain. To fix this, place 2 drops of glycerine on an old toothbrush and lightly brush across the surface of the carpet. Be careful not to push the glycerine into the backing of the carpet

or it will release more tannins. Leave for 90 minutes. Tightly wring a cloth in white vinegar. Hold it flat against the stained area and polish out the stain as though polishing a table. Make sure you don't push your fingers into the carpet. If you can't see the urine, in a darkened room, turn on an ultraviolet light and the urine stains will show up yellow. Mark around the yellow stains with white chalk so you can identify where the stain is. Then remove the urine stain with white vinegar on a cloth. In all cases, absorb moisture by covering the area with paper towel and standing on it. Continue to change the paper towel until it's no longer wet when you stand on it. If you need to repeat, wait 24 hours.

Urine on timber

Q: 'We live on the edge of bushland and love the tranquillity but our deck has become a bit of a haven for rabbits,' reports Ben. 'The particular problem is rabbit urine staining the timber. How can we get it out?'

Problem:	**Rabbit urine on timber**
What to use:	**White vinegar, brush; plaster of Paris, water, white vinegar**

How to apply: Remove by scrubbing with white vinegar on a stiff brush. If the urine has penetrated into the timber, mix plaster of Paris and water to the consistency of peanut butter. For each cup of mixture, add 2 teaspoons of white vinegar. Spread 6 mm to 1.3 cm thick over the stain with the brush. Allow to dry completely. If it feels cold on the back of your hand, it's not dry. When dry, crack it with the back of the brush and brush away.

 To deter unwanted rabbits, add 1 teaspoon of Vicks VapoRub, 1 teaspoon of naphthalene flakes or 2 mothballs to 1 litre of water in a spray pack. Don't soak the area – mist it.

Grooming

Rabbits are good groomers and don't require weekly bathing. But when a new coat is growing or they lose their old one, a bath will help to remove muck. Short-haired rabbits should be brushed with a fine-bristled brush every week. Long-haired rabbits should be brushed every day to avoid matting. Because rabbit skin is fine and soft, don't use a stiff brush.

 Some rabbits like to swim in lukewarm water. It helps with grooming.

Problem: **Rabbit hair on upholstery**
What to use: **Disposable rubber gloves, cake of bathroom soap, water**
How to apply: Put on a pair of disposable rubber gloves and wash your gloved hands with a cake of bathroom soap and water. Shake your hands dry and then wipe over the hair. It will stick to the gloves.

 Save rabbit hair to make wool or felt. To clean it, boil a pot of water on the stove, place an open-weave cloth, preferably cotton or linen, over the top of the pot and lay the hair on top of the cloth. The steam will clean the hair and compact it, making it easier to spin.

Sleeping

If your rabbit is indoors, create a zone for your bunny that includes a dark, enclosed area in which it can hide and sleep. If possible, remove electrical cords from the rabbit's reach, because rabbits like to chew. In a corner of the enclosed area, set up a litter tray filled with straw and clean it every day. Rabbits produce a shovel-sized amount of poo in a day, so if your bunny lives inside, ensure there's an accessible and appropriately sized poo tray and clean it daily.

If your rabbit is outdoors, the hutch should be high enough for the rabbit to stand on its hind legs. Cover the base with straw and clean it each week, or more often if dirty. Cover open areas of the hutch with flyscreen to protect your rabbit from mosquitoes.

Whether located outside or inside, it's important to keep hutches clean. When cleaning, remove the contents of the hutch, including uneaten food, sweep the floor with a brush or broom and wipe surfaces with a damp cloth. To remove urine stains, wipe with white vinegar on a cloth. If the hutch is outside, wash it using a hose. If it has a wire base and is kept on lawn, keep moving it around. Hose over the old area to break down faeces and residue, and if the grass is long, check for snakes. Rabbit hutches can also attract rats because of food residue. Deter rats by sprinkling naphthalene flakes in a circle outside the rabbit enclosure.

 Don't use ammonia-based cleaners around rabbits. Urine also contains ammonia, so ammonia-based cleaners will encourage your rabbit to return to this spot to pee.

Play

Rabbits like to play. Keep them entertained with toys such as willow balls or items they can carry in their paws. Exercise is also important. Rabbits like to dig and play in sand, which keeps their claws in good condition and means they are less likely to scratch you.

If you want to see a happy rabbit in action, punch the words 'binky bunny' into YouTube and watch the crazy jumping and careening activities.

GUINEA PIGS

Guinea pigs are often chosen as pets for children because they are small, cuddly and easy to care for. But they can be quite messy.

Feeding

Guinea pigs eat grass, food pellets, hay, fruit and vegetables and particularly enjoy the tops of carrots. Don't feed them onions or citrus fruits.

Guinea pig poo is small and easy to remove. Guinea pig urine, on the other hand, is very acidic. Fortunately, guinea pigs can be toilet-trained.

Problem:	**Guinea pig urine on carpet**
What to use:	**Ultraviolet light, white chalk, cloth, white vinegar; glycerine, old toothbrush; paper towel**
How to apply:	First find where the urine is. In a darkened room, turn on an ultraviolet light and the urine stains will show up yellow. Mark around the yellow stains with a piece of white chalk so you know where to clean. Wipe inside the chalk marks with a cloth tightly wrung in white vinegar. If the urine has penetrated to the back of the carpet, the jute releases a tannin stain. To fix this, place 2 drops of glycerine on an old toothbrush and lightly brush across the surface of the carpet. Be

careful not to push the glycerine into the backing of the carpet or it will release more tannins. Leave for 90 minutes. Tightly wring a cloth in white vinegar. Hold it flat against the stained area and polish out as though polishing a table. Make sure you don't push your fingers into the carpet. If stain remains, leave 24 hours before repeating. In all cases, absorb moisture by covering the area with paper towel and stand on it. Continue to change the paper towel until it's no longer wet when you stand on it.

Problem: **Guinea pig urine on tiles and other hard surfaces**

What to use: **White vinegar, cloth; plaster of Paris, water, brush**

How to apply: Guinea pig urine can remove the polish on hard surfaces and etch tiles and grout. Clean the urine as soon as possible by wiping with white vinegar on a cloth. If the stain has penetrated through tiles or grout, mix plaster of Paris and water to the consistency of peanut butter. To each cup of mixture, add 2 teaspoons of white vinegar. Spread 6 mm to 1.3 cm thick over the stain with a brush. Allow to dry completely. If it feels cold on the back of your hand, it's not dry. When dry, crack with the back of the brush and sweep away.

TIP Don't be alarmed if your guinea pig eats its own poo. This is known as coprophagia and it helps to maintain good bacteria in their digestive tract. It could indicate they are missing certain bacteria from their diet. Ensure there's variety in their diet with plenty of green feed in the mix.

Problem: **Guinea pig diarrhoea on carpet/ upholstery**

What to use: **Plastic comb, paper towel, talcum powder, cake of bathroom soap, cold water, pantyhose; dishwashing liquid, cloth**

How to apply: Guinea pig diarrhoea is very acidic. Remove excess by lifting the solids with a plastic comb or by blotting liquids with paper towel. Create an edge around the stain with either talcum powder or paper towel. Scribble over the stained area with a cake of bathroom soap dipped in cold water as if using a crayon. Work from the outside to the inside of the stain. Wipe with damp pantyhose rolled in a ball. If any stain remains, massage with 2 drops of dishwashing liquid on your fingertips until the liquid feels like jelly. Wipe with a damp cloth until the dishwashing liquid is removed. In all cases, absorb moisture by covering the area with paper towel and standing on it. Continue to change the paper towel until it's no longer wet when you stand on it.

Grooming

If you have a long-haired guinea pig, brush it each day with a soft brush. If it has fleas, wash with cold mint tea. To create this mix, add 2 teaspoons of dried mint or 4 teaspoons of fresh mint to 240 ml of hot water. Allow the tea to steep for at least 15 minutes and strain. Allow it to cool. Then add it to the wash water. If you see black spots resembling fleas in your guinea pig's coat, they could be mites. Consult your vet immediately.

Enclosures/hutches

Guinea pigs should be kept in a large enclosure with shredded paper, soft straw or fleece along the base. Change the base material every day to avoid ammonia build-up from guinea pig urine. Never use cedar shavings because the fragrant oils are dangerous for guinea pigs' respiratory systems. Include a darkened section in the enclosure because guinea pigs like to burrow and nest. They prefer soft bedding in their hutch. A guinea pig enclosure must have a solid base to prevent foot injury in your piggy. Guinea pigs also need time out of their enclosure and love to run. Provide toys for them to chew on and a running wheel.

Clean enclosures every 3 days or you'll have a nasty smell. Wipe with white vinegar on a cloth. To deter bugs, wipe the interior with 2 drops of lemon oil and 5 drops of lavender oil on a cloth. Secure flyscreen to outdoor hutches to protect your guinea pig from bugs. Regularly clean food containers and change water every day or algae will grow. When cleaning bowls, don't use detergents but sprinkle with a small amount of salt and rub with pantyhose. The salt acts as a mild abrasive. Rinse with clean water. The bowl must be dry or it will quickly go mouldy.

Because guinea pigs love to run, set up an extra enclosure outside. Make your own by moulding chicken wire into a tube shape. Then they can run free with protection.

Portable guinea pig carriers are usually covered in removable polyester material with removable floor matting that can be cleaned in the washing machine.

DID YOU KNOW? Some people are allergic to guinea pigs. The allergic reaction is not to hair, but to proteins in guinea pigs' urine and saliva.

 TIP Keep your guinea pig cool on hot days. It doesn't cope well with heat. One option is to place frozen water bottles or frozen blocks covered with towels or sterilisation wrap in the hutch.

Problem:	**Soiled fleece/fabric bedding**
What to use:	**Bucket/tub, blood-heat (body temperature) water, white vinegar, cake of bathroom soap, sunshine/clothes airer**
How to apply:	Place fleece or bedding in a bucket or tub along with blood-heat (body temperature) water and 2 cups of white vinegar. Leave to soak overnight. Wash with a cake of bathroom soap and blood-heat water. Rinse in blood-heat water. Dry fabric in sunshine and fleece on a clothes airer in the shade.

TIP If guinea pigs are happy, they make a high-pitched sound. If their teeth are chattering, it indicates stress. If you hear a single high-pitched squeak, consult your vet.

RATS AND MICE

Rats have a bad reputation mainly because of their association with disease and plagues. They've been demonised in literature including the novel *1984* and popular TV show *Game of Thrones*. But there's a big difference between the rats found in sewers and the ones you buy from breeders. Owners say rats and mice are cuddly and intelligent animals and even respond when you call their name. Perhaps this explains why Mickey Mouse is the world's most famous cartoon character.

Feeding

Most rats and mice eat grains and vegetables. They'll eat dog food and eggs if they can get their paws onto them.

Problem:	**Rat/mouse urine on carpet**
What to use:	**Ultraviolet light, white chalk, cloth, white vinegar; glycerine, old toothbrush; paper towel**
How to apply:	First find where the urine is. In a darkened room, turn on an ultraviolet light and the urine stains will show up yellow. Mark around the yellow stains with a piece of white chalk so you can see where to clean. Wipe inside the chalk marks with a cloth tightly wrung

in white vinegar. If the urine has penetrated to the back of the carpet, the jute releases a tannin stain. To fix this, place 2 drops of glycerine on an old toothbrush and lightly brush across the surface of the carpet. Be careful not to push the glycerine into the backing of the carpet or it will release more tannins. Leave for 90 minutes. Tightly wring a cloth in white vinegar. Hold it flat against the stained area and polish the stain out as though polishing a table. Make sure you don't push your fingers into the carpet. If stain remains, leave 24 hours before repeating. In all cases, absorb moisture by covering the area with paper towel and standing on it. Continue to change the paper towel until it's no longer wet when you stand on it.

Problem: **Greasy rat/mouse poo on carpet**

What to use: **Cake of bathroom soap, cold water, cloth, dishwashing liquid, bucket, paper towel**

How to apply: Because rats are omnivores, their poo is greasy, leaving a yellow–brown mark and a nasty smell. Scribble with a cake of bathroom soap dipped in cold water as though using a crayon. Wipe with a damp cloth. To remove the greasy mark, mix dishwashing liquid and cold water in a bucket to create a sudsy mix and wipe the suds only over the stain with a cloth. Rinse by wiping with a damp cloth. If the area still smells, repeat. Absorb moisture by covering the area with paper towel and standing on it. Continue to change the paper towel until it's no longer wet when you stand on it.

 TIP Rats have one set of teeth throughout their life that grow continuously and chewing keeps their teeth aligned and trimmed. Give them something to gnaw on, such as stainless steel wool, or timber, and replace as needed. There are many chewing toys available in pet stores or online.

Cages

Keep rats in a wire cage, because they enjoy climbing and a cage allows good ventilation. Keep the cage away from draughts – rats are prone to catching colds – and ensure there is a dark area in the cage for the rats to sleep in. Mice are able to live in smaller plastic cages. Mice and rat cages should be cleaned every day to combat nasty odours from urine that can spread throughout the house. Clean with equal parts white vinegar and water. Replace newspaper or shredded straw each day. Clean feeding bowls every day in dishwashing liquid and hot water. Because rats like to chew, place flyscreen on the outside of the wire. Prevent chewing by adding 1 teaspoon of Vicks VapoRub, 1 teaspoon of naphthalene flakes or 2 mothballs to 1 litre of water in a spray pack. Spray the mixture on a cloth and wipe the cloth over the area.

Rats and mice like to hang upside down and enjoy climbing on toy ladders. Mouse wheels and mazes are also favourites. Even old tissue boxes can be converted into playhouses.

 If the rat or mouse goes outside, it may come into contact with other animals and pick up disease. Before returning them to their inside cage, spray with diluted lavender oil. Mix 1 teaspoon of lavender oil in a 1-litre spray pack of water. Don't forget to wipe over their paws.

 Male rats like to be cuddled more than female rats.

> **Problem:** **Rat/mouse hair on the couch**
> **What to use:** **Disposable rubber gloves, cake of bathroom soap, water**
> **How to apply:** Put on a pair of disposable rubber gloves and wash your gloved hands with a cake of bathroom soap and water. Shake your hands dry and then wipe over the hair. It will stick to the gloves.

FERRETS

Ferrets are described as intelligent and playful pets but are illegal to keep in Queensland, the ACT and the Northern Territory. Ferrets are carnivores and have the same cleaning issues as cats and dogs. And while they get on with cats or dogs, they don't with birds, fish, rabbits, rodents or lizards.

Feeding

Ferrets are carnivores and eat chicken necks and wings, rabbits and quails. They also need calcium from bones. Fresh water should be available at all times. Use a large, heavy feeding bowl so they can't tip it over. Ferrets like to hide food, and if yours runs free around the house, you could discover old food in odd locations.

Problem:	**Ferret poo on carpet**
What to use:	**Plastic comb/paper towel, cake of bathroom soap, cold water; old toothbrush/pantyhose, vacuum cleaner; or plastic comb/paper towel, bucket, cold water, dishwashing liquid; paper towel**
How to apply:	Remove excess by lifting the solids with a plastic comb or blotting liquids with paper towel. Scribble with a cake of bathroom soap dipped in cold water as if using a crayon. If the stain is stubborn, scrub with an old toothbrush or pantyhose. Leave to dry. Vacuum. Alternatively, remove excess then fill a bucket with cold water and enough dishwashing liquid to generate a sudsy mix. Apply only the suds with a toothbrush, using as little water as possible. In all cases, absorb moisture by covering the area with paper towel and standing on it. Continue to change the paper towel until it's no longer wet when you stand on it.

Problem:	**Ferret urine on carpet**
What to use:	**Ultraviolet light, white chalk, white vinegar, old toothbrush/cloth; glycerine; paper towel**
How to apply:	In a darkened room, turn on an ultraviolet light and the urine stains will show up yellow. Mark around the yellow stains with a piece of white chalk so you can see where to clean. Wipe with white vinegar on either an old toothbrush or a tightly wrung cloth. Repeat if needed. If the urine has penetrated to the back of the carpet, the jute releases a tannin stain. To fix this, place 2 drops of glycerine on an old toothbrush and lightly brush across the surface of the carpet. Be careful not to push the glycerine into the back of the carpet or it will release more tannins. Leave for 90 minutes. Tightly wring a cloth in white vinegar. Hold it flat against the stained area and polish out as though polishing a table. Make sure you don't push your fingers into the carpet. Leave for 24 hours. In all cases, absorb moisture by covering the area with paper towel and standing on it. Continue to change the paper towel until it's no longer wet when you stand on it.

Enclosures

Ensure there is enough room for the ferret to run around. Small areas will stifle their need to run. Keep straw in the base of the enclosure and change it every day. Ferrets go to the toilet in corners by instinct and can be trained to use a litter tray. Ferret bedding is available at pet stores and can be washed in the washing machine, or use an old towel. Clean bedding weekly – twice weekly during shedding seasons. Ferrets also need a darkened area to sleep in such as a sack, hammock or old T-shirt.

 Ferrets are particularly sensitive to detergents, fabric softeners and commercial household cleaners. Use low-toxic cleaners.

Grooming

The ferret is part of the mink family and has a very soft coat. Each spring and autumn, ferrets cast off their coats, releasing musk oils that stink. To get rid of the smell, you need to remove every bit of loose hair from the house and from them.

Ferrets are good groomers and don't need regular baths but can be washed if they've rolled in something horrible. They do need their ears to be cleaned and nails clipped. They're also susceptible to fleas. A natural solution, as long as the ferret or women in the house are not pregnant, is to apply 2 drops of oil of pennyroyal between the ferret's ears and down the back of their neck every 2 weeks.

⚠ WARNING

*Don't use oil of pennyroyal if your ferret or women in the house
are pregnant.*

 While moulting, ferrets like to rub against cat towers,
so towers will need to be de-furred afterwards.

Problem: **Ferret hair on carpet**

What to use: **Condom, broom, cake of bathroom soap,
water, bucket, vacuum cleaner**

How to apply: Ferret hair is difficult to remove from carpet.
The best method is to use a condom. Place
the condom over the bristles of a soft broom,
wash it with a cake of bathroom soap and
water, air-dry and sweep over the carpet. Keep
a bucket filled with water on hand to rinse as
you go, making sure you don't get water on
the carpet. Vacuum.

Problem: **Ferret hair on upholstery**

What to use: **Disposable rubber gloves, cake of
bathroom soap, water**

How to apply: Put on a pair of disposable rubber gloves
and wash your gloved hands with a cake of
bathroom soap and water. Shake your hands
dry and then wipe over the hair. It will stick to
the gloves.

Travelling

Ferrets can be walked with a harness and lead. Just be aware that dogs and magpies may attack them. If taking them in the car, use a cat cage and have water and food available for them.

HERMIT CRABS

Hermit crabs carry around discarded snail shells to protect their abdomen, and they move from them as they grow. When keeping hermit crabs, ensure there are several shells of different sizes for them to move into. Buy shells from the pet shop because then they'll be sterilised. Boiling a spiral shell is difficult. Whatever you do, never release hermit crabs into the wild.

When the hermit crab moults, it discards its outer skeleton and then eats it. When this happens, it drinks more water and often burrows into the gravel. Don't touch the crab during moulting and ensure there's plenty of food and water for it.

 TIP Be careful using fly sprays and household cleaners near hermit crabs. They are very sensitive to chemicals.

Tanks/enclosures

Hermit crabs are tropical and need to be housed in a temperature of between 26 and 32 degrees Celsius. An aquarium with a glass top is ideal. Include a hidey hut for them to escape to and hide in. Cover the floor with gravel, pet litter or dry wood shavings. When you see algae or poo, clean it with hot salty water – never detergents. To clean gravel, remove it from the aquarium and place it in a sieve. Put a bucket underneath the sieve and flush with boiling water. Repeat until clean. Allow the gravel to dry then put it back inside the tank. There can be a small amount of moisture in the gravel. To clean the tank, wipe over the inside of the glass with pantyhose – wrap the pantyhose over your hand to create a mitt.

 Ensure there are 2 bowls of water for hermit crabs – 1 with fresh water for drinking and another with salt water for bathing.

TURTLES

If you work long hours, a turtle could be the ideal pet for you. The most common types of pet turtle are the Eastern snake-necked turtle and the long-necked turtle. In Australia, you need a licence to keep a native or freshwater turtle – contact the National Parks and Wildlife Service in your State or Territory for details. It's against the law to remove a turtle from the wild.

Feeding

Australian freshwater turtles are carnivorous and eat food pellets and fresh fish, insects and worms. Turtles often regurgitate their food.

Problem: Turtle vomit (meat) on carpet/upholstery

What to use: Plastic comb/paper towel, cake of bathroom soap, cold water, damp cloth, glycerine, old toothbrush, white vinegar, cloth

How to apply: Remove excess by lifting the solids with a plastic comb or by blotting liquids with paper towel. Scribble with a cake of bathroom soap dipped in cold water. Wipe with a damp cloth. To remove stomach acids, lightly brush with 2 drops of glycerine on an old toothbrush. Leave for 90 minutes. Tightly wring a cloth in white vinegar. Hold it flat against the stained area and polish out as though polishing a table. Absorb moisture by covering the area with paper towel and standing on it. Continue to change the paper towel until it's no longer wet when you stand on it.

Problem: Turtle vomit (vegetable) on carpet/upholstery

What to use: White vinegar, old toothbrush/cloth, glycerine, paper towel, oil of cloves

How to apply: Turtles enjoy chewing vegetables that can rot and stain carpet when regurgitated. If this happens, wipe with white vinegar on an old toothbrush or tightly wrung damp cloth. To fix the tannin stain, place 2 drops of glycerine on an old toothbrush and lightly brush across the surface of the carpet. Be careful not to push the glycerine into the backing of the carpet or it will release more tannins. Leave for 90 minutes. Tightly wring a cloth in white vinegar. Hold it flat against the stained area and polish out as though polishing a table. Make sure you don't push your fingers into the carpet. If stain remains, leave 24 hours before repeating. In all cases, absorb moisture by covering the area with paper towel and standing on it. Continue to change the paper towel until it's no longer wet when you stand on it. To inhibit mould, wipe 1 drop of oil of cloves over the clean area using your fingertips.

Turtles can't be toilet-trained. If they begin to poo while you're holding them, quickly put something under them to catch it.

Problem: **Turtle poo on carpet**
What to use: **Cake of bathroom soap, cold water, cloth, dishwashing liquid, bucket, paper towel**
How to apply: Turtle poo is greasy and smelly. Wipe with a cake of bathroom soap and cold water on a cloth. To remove the greasy mark, mix dishwashing liquid and cold water in a bucket to create a sudsy mix and wipe the suds only over the stain with a cloth. Rinse by wiping

with a damp cloth. If it still smells, repeat. Absorb moisture by covering the area with paper towel and stand on it. Continue to change the paper towel until it's no longer wet when you stand on it.

 TIP If your turtle doesn't finish its food, remove the uneaten food from the enclosure and feed it smaller portions.

Tanks/enclosures

Baby turtles should be kept indoors in an aquarium or enclosure that has a pond inside. Older turtles can be kept outdoors in a tank, except during the winter when they hibernate and need warmth. Clean turtle tanks or enclosures weekly. Wipe over the inside of the glass with damp pantyhose over your hand like a mitt. Wipe the outside of the tank with white vinegar on a cloth. Never use strong detergents. Remove poo every day and regularly change the water.

Turtles need exposure to 12 hours of light a day from a UV lamp and require constant supervision when out of their enclosure because they can crawl under fences quite easily. Some need both dry land and an area for swimming – consult your vet. Freshwater turtles need to be able to submerge themselves in water in order to eat. The pH level and temperature of the water have to be carefully monitored. The ideal temperature range is between 21 and 32 degrees Celsius.

SNAKES

In Britain, pet reptiles outnumber pet dogs, the most popular reptiles being snakes, geckoes and bearded dragons. (The figures are calculated through sales of reptile food, including mice and insects.) In Australia, you need a licence to keep a snake and should follow specific guidelines on how they are to be housed and cared for. Advice for snakes applies to other reptiles.

Enclosures

The size of your snake's enclosure will be determined by the size of the snake – if the enclosure is too big, the snake will feel stressed. Line the base of the enclosure with gravel, mulch, rocks and branches that most closely match their natural environment. Include a hiding area. Reptiles need a heating system to regulate their temperature. Ensure there is a range of temperatures or heat gradient along the base of the enclosure so they can seek warmer and cooler temperatures. This means placing different heating pads under the tank that have different temperatures. It's also a good idea to have a lid on the enclosure so the snake can't slither out. Ensure there is plenty of clean water for drinking. Venomous snakes have to be kept in secure enclosures under a Class 2 licence. There's also a Class 3 licence for species that are difficult to keep or rare in the wild.

Cleaning enclosures

Clean once a week or whenever there's poo. When cleaning,
place your snake in another enclosure or a pillowcase. Remove
the contents of the enclosure and wash. Replace shavings
or leaf matter – use old leaf matter as mulch in the garden.
Because snakes are territorial, the mulch will repel other
snakes. Wipe diluted white vinegar over the inside of the glass
with pantyhose over your hand. Ensure the white vinegar
isn't too strong because snakeskin is very absorbent and soft,
particularly after shedding. Remove excess by wiping with
paper towel. Replace contents and your reptile.

 Save snake poo. It deters mice and possums.

 Snakes shed their skin each month. If your snake hasn't
eaten the discarded skin after a few days, remove it from
the enclosure.

SPIDERS

While many people are scared of spiders, others find them
fascinating and love keeping them as pets. Admittedly, they
fall into the 'extreme pet' category. They come in a variety
of shapes and colours; naturally, you should avoid highly
venomous varieties. Popular Australian spiders include the
St Andrew's Cross, garden orb weaver, jumping spider and
wolf spider. Before keeping a spider as a pet, research their
behaviour. Choose hunters rather than web builders.

A spider eats insects such as flies or crickets, or larger animals, twice a week depending on its size. Don't handle spiders because it damages the delicate hairs that help them to judge distances and determine what's around them.

Enclosures

Depending on the type and size of the spider, house it in a glass jar with a lid with holes in it, or an aquarium or terrarium containing gravel or soil, sticks and plants. Add wet paper towel or cotton to maintain humidity. Make your own terrarium from a used clean soft-drink bottle. Clean it once a week.

DID YOU KNOW? Spider webs have been used to make fabrics, and as an adhesive, a natural antibiotic and a blood coagulator. For centuries, spider webs were used to staunch swordfight wounds. They have even been dubbed 'webicillin'.

NATIVE ANIMALS

Laws about keeping native animals as pets are determined by the States and Territories. For a handy outline of current rules and regulations, consult the Australian Veterinary Association (AVA).[6]

In most States you need a licence to keep native animals as pets. In New South Wales, for example, dingos, spinifex hopping mice and plains rats are the only mammals that can be kept as pets. There is a push, however, for changes to these

6   www.ava.com.au/policy/64-native-animals-pets

rules. Those against the push argue that because most native animals are nocturnal, interaction with humans isn't ideal. But those in favour claim it would lead to wonderful interaction with native animals and increased awareness of the need to protect native species.

Professor Michael Archer, from the University of New South Wales, wrote about his experience of keeping a quoll as a pet: 'He was obsessively clean, never failing to use a box of kitty litter for all excretions, dog-like in his love of play throughout his life. Bright and quick to learn, far more affectionate and attentive than a cat, intently curious, happy to play on his own but clearly happier to play with me, active particularly in the late afternoons and evenings and asleep at more or less the same times as me, puppy-like when playing even as an adult, careful to mouth without biting, content to fall asleep in my lap, generally very quiet with only "purring", clicks or "nark!" sounds rather than yowls or barks, no "spraying" or other stinky habits, and generally fascinating.'[7]

Possums

While debate continues around keeping native animals as pets, some native animals come uninvited in our homes. A common guest is the possum. If you want to deter possums, which can make noisy, scratchy sounds in the roof, wipe a little Vicks VapoRub around doors and windows. To keep possums out of ceiling cavities, leave a few mothballs or naphthalene flakes inside the ceiling cavity, around doors, windows, vents and

---

7   www.abc.net.au/environment/articles/2015/03/19/4200500.htm

eaves. To keep possums out of your garden, put a little Vicks VapoRub on a stone or stones, turn them face down to the ground and place them in the garden. Turning the stone over prevents rain from washing the Vicks away.

 Possums love to eat citrus fruit. To protect the fruit, wipe Vicks VapoRub around the base of the tree.

 If you enjoy interacting with nature, there are steps you can take to encourage creatures into your yard. Certain flowers and plants invite particular birds or butterflies. A garden pond could encourage frogs of different stripes and spots to visit. It's quite wonderful to hear the croaking sound of frogs at dusk.

Flying foxes

Q: 'Flying fox poo landed on my new canvas tent,' says Nathan. 'What should I do?'

Problem:	**Yellow or purple flying fox poo on canvas**
What to use:	**Cake of bathroom soap, cold water, white vinegar, cloth; glycerine; brush; non-iodised salt, bucket, water**
How to apply:	If coloured purple, wipe with a cake of bathroom soap and cold water, then wipe with white vinegar on a cloth. If coloured yellow, orange or brown, wipe with glycerine first, leave for 90 minutes, then wipe with soap and

cold water. Flying fox poo is high in tannins and protein. Remove by dipping a cake of bathroom soap in cold water, rubbing it over the bristles of a stiff brush and scrubbing. When the stain is removed, make the canvas waterproof by mixing 1 kilo of non-iodised salt in a 9-litre bucket of water. Saturate the canvas with the salt solution and hang to dry. When dry, remove the salt.

TIP To deter flying foxes, hang old CDs or DVDs with fishing line. Flying foxes don't like unusual movement or shiny reflections.

Q: 'There's flying fox poo on my garage roller door,' reports Charlie. 'How can I get it off?

Problem:	**Flying fox poo on powder-coated steel**
What to use:	**Dishwashing liquid, cold water, pantyhose, glycerine, cloth**
How to apply:	Remove as quickly as possible because the poo can etch the surface. Apply 2 of drops of dishwashing liquid and cold water to pantyhose and wipe over the stain. Then wipe with glycerine on a cloth. If needed, repeat after 24 hours.

DID YOU KNOW? In 1975, Gary Dahl had an idea for the 'perfect' pet: a rock. Created from a smooth stone with googly eyes glued on, pet rocks were delivered in a customised box with breathing holes, straw and an official training manual. They were popular for about 6 months, but interest then waned. They became available for sale again in September 2012.

PESTS

It's a bit harder to keep pests at bay in the outdoors than in the home. Here are some natural solutions to deter common barbecue-stoppers.

Mosquitoes – Lavender oil is a great mozzie deterrent. Place a couple of drops on a cloth and wipe around outdoor chairs and tables. Alternatively, place 1 teaspoon of lavender oil in a 1-litre spray pack of water and lightly mist around the area. You can also rub lavender oil directly onto your wrists. Plant lavender, basil, pennyroyal (except if anyone is pregnant), pelargonium citrosum (citronella plant) or tansy around entertainment areas. If there's water in the base of pot plants, add a couple of drops of lavender oil to inhibit mozzies.

Spiders – Spiders hate lemon oil. Add a couple of drops of lemon oil to the head of a broom, or rub the outside of a lemon rind over it, and sweep over areas where spiders lurk. Don't forget bins, shed shelves and tools. Repeat every 3 months. To reach spiders under the house, mix ¼ teaspoon of lemon oil in a 1-litre spray pack of water and squirt through vents and around access areas. To make lemon oil, take plastic wrap and lay it flat on a bench. Zest lemon skin onto the wrap and lay the plastic on the windowsill in the sunshine. After 24 to 48 hours, little beads of oil will form on the plastic. The lemon zest will go black. Lightly dust the black bits away. You'll get 2 to 4 drops of oil per lemon. Put the oil in a bottle as you go. The zest will also give the room a fresh lemon smell.

Flies – To kill flies, put white or black pepper (not red or green) onto a piece of paper painted with sugar and water. The sugar attracts the flies and the pepper kills them. Pepper contains piperine which is a toxin to flies.

Ants – Mix equal parts powdered borax and icing sugar for sweet ants, or equal parts powdered borax and grated parmesan cheese for savoury ants. Or find their nest and pour boiling water down it. To find an ants' nest, sprinkle talcum powder where you see ants and they will track the powder back to their nest. Just follow the white trail. Ants are attracted to animal hutches. Pouring boiling water down their nest is the safest method.

⚠ WARNING

Borax is toxic and should not be placed where children or pets could eat it.

Snails/slugs – Wipe petroleum jelly (Vaseline) around areas where snails and slugs wander – they won't cross it. Renew every couple of months. Protect plants by crushing a clove of garlic into a 1-litre spray pack of water. Allow it to steep for 2 hours, strain and spray over plants. To make a trap for snails, cut an orange in half, remove the flesh and half-fill both orange skins with beer. The snails will be attracted by the beer and climb in then won't be able to get out. If you have a mouldy bathroom, the solution could be a few slugs slithering across the tiles and grout. Trialled by Martyn Robinson from the Australian Museum, the best mould-removing variety is the limax flava. Make a little house for them in an upturned flower pot. They roam at night and prefer cold rather than warm environments.

Fruit flies – What to do will depend on how big the infestation is. Use a glass jar with a plastic or metal lid. Punch holes at 2 mm intervals in the lid. Half-fill the jar with 1 tablespoon of Vegemite and ½ cup of white vinegar. Tie string around the jar and hang it from a tree or branch. Fruit flies will be attracted to the yeast and acetic mix, fly into the jar through the holes and become trapped. Once you have an infestation, it's time for what Shannon calls the 'fruit fly dance'. Make your own butterfly net. To do this, open a coat hanger to form a loop and attach a stick to the straightened hook. Sew fine tulle to the open circle to create a net. Every morning and evening, catch as many fruit flies as you can in the net. Then spray with lavender oil spray. Kill the flies by stomping on the net with your feet. To get the infestation under control, do this for 3 days.

CHAPTER 7

A–Z STAIN REMOVAL

ALGAE

On birdbath

- Remove water from the birdbath and wipe over the surface with a rolled-up pair of pantyhose. To prevent the problem from recurring, add a pinch of non-iodised salt to each litre of clean water. Birds won't be deterred by the tiny amount of salt, but algae will.

On canvas/pavers/vinyl

- Mix 2 tablespoons of copper sulphate solution in a 9-litre bucket of hot or cold water.
- Sweep the mixture over the surface with a brush or broom.
- Allow to dry. It will blow away in a couple of days.
- For vinyl, wipe with 2 drops of glycerine on a cloth. Leave for 24 hours. Then follow instructions above.

On fish tank glass

- Wipe over the inside of the glass with pantyhose pulled over your hand like a mitt.

AQUARIUM

(see FISH TANK)

BIRD POO

On cage wire

- Wipe with a cake of bathroom soap and cold water on a cloth.
- Wipe with white vinegar on a cloth.
- To protect from corrosion, wipe with sweet almond oil or vegetable oil on a cloth.

On a car

- Remove as soon as possible by wiping with a damp cloth.
- If the poo has hardened, leave a damp cloth over the poo for 10 minutes to soften it. Then wipe clean.
- To remove dullness in the duco, polish with equal parts glycerine and talcum powder on a rolled-up pair of pantyhose.

On fabric/upholstery

- For seed-eating birds, wipe with a cake of bathroom soap and cold water on lightly dampened pantyhose. Clean the entire panel in even, parallel strokes or you'll get a watermark.
- Bird poo can shrink leather. After removing, wipe with leather conditioner. Make your own by placing 1 teaspoon of beeswax, 1 teaspoon of lavender oil and 1 teaspoon of lemon oil on a 100 per cent cotton cloth, such as an old T-shirt. Place in the microwave in a microwave-safe dish. Microwave on high in 10-second bursts until the beeswax

melts. After using the cloth, place it in a zip-lock bag and store in the freezer ready to use again.

- For meat-eating birds, wipe stain with a cake of bathroom soap and cold water.
- For fish and insect eaters, the poo will penetrate deeply and needs to be cleaned thoroughly because it can attract maggots. After wiping with a cake of bathroom soap and cold water, rub dishwashing liquid into the spot with your fingers until it feels like jelly and wipe with a damp cloth.
- For birds that eat fruit, including berries, apples and oranges, wipe stain with glycerine, leave for 90 minutes, then wipe with a cake of bathroom soap and water.
- For yellow residue, wipe with lavender oil on a cloth then wipe with a damp cloth.

On glass

- Mix 1 tablespoon of glycerine and 1 litre of water in a spray pack.
- When the glass is cold, spray over the mixture and wipe with a damp cloth.
- If the glass is cloudy, wipe with sweet almond oil.

On outdoor furniture/railings

- For painted surfaces, rub a cake of bathroom soap over the head of a soft, clean broom, add cold water and scrub over the poo. If the stain has set, wipe with glycerine, leave for 90 minutes, then follow the above method. Avoid using detergents and, if possible, clean in the shade.

- For oiled timber, clean with a cake of bathroom soap and cold water. You may need to clean the entire panel. After removing the stain, re-oil the timber. If there are bleach marks, wipe with strong black tea.
- For powder-coated surfaces, wipe with cold water and a cake of bathroom soap on a cloth. Alternatively, make a paste of glycerine and talcum powder, place over the stain and leave for up to 1 hour. Then remove with rolled-up pantyhose. If the stain has etched the coating, wipe the entire item or rail with sweet almond oil.
- For surfaces coated in rust-proof paint, wipe with a cake of bathroom soap and cold water on a cloth then wipe with white spirits on a cloth.
- For raw metal, wipe with bicarb and white vinegar. If dulled, polish the section with jeweller's rouge using a sheepskin buff on an electric drill. Some painted metal finishes will need to be retouched.

BIRTHING

When a pet gives birth, it makes a big mess and is difficult to clean because it contains amniotic sac, blood and urea.

On carpet/upholstery

- The carpet will need to be lifted because you need access to both sides of it – you can't just clean the surface.
- Scribble with a cake of bathroom soap dipped in cold water as if using a crayon.

- Wipe with a cloth tightly wrung out in white vinegar.
- Remove tannin stains by wiping with 2 drops of glycerine on an old toothbrush. Leave for 90 minutes. Then wipe with a damp cloth.

On leather shoes

- If inside leather shoes, sprinkle with talcum powder and allow to dry.
- Remove as much as possible.
- Wipe a cloth with a cake of bathroom soap and cold water and clean inside the shoe.
- When drying, place scrunched-up newspaper inside to keep the shape of the shoes.

On timber/pavers

- Mix equal parts plaster of Paris and talcum powder. For every 3 cups of mixture, add 2 tablespoons of grated soap or soap flakes.
- Paint the mixture 6 mm to 1.3 cm thick onto the stain with a brush and allow it to dry completely. If it feels cold on the back of your hand, it's not dry.
- When dry, crack it with the back of the brush and sweep clean.

BLANKET

To clean

- For wool, wash with 1 teaspoon of cheap shampoo in 9 litres of blood-heat (body temperature) water.

- Rinse with 1 teaspoon of cheap hair conditioner in 9 litres of blood-heat water.
- For polar fleece, acrylic and cotton, wash in the washing machine with laundry detergent.
- In all cases, dry on the clothesline pegged in a U shape. Place a sheet over the top to protect the fibres from the sun.

BLOOD

Blood is a protein stain and can be removed with cold water and a cake of bathroom soap. Don't use detergents or heat because they set the stain.

On carpet/upholstery

- If you used foam upholstery cleaner or commercial spray to clean the stain, neutralise first by wiping with white vinegar on a cloth. If you used liquid carpet cleaner, neutralise first by rubbing with unprocessed wheat bran. When neutralised, brush with 2 drops of glycerine on an old toothbrush and leave for 90 minutes. If the sofa contains horsehair or jute, the moisture can release a tannin stain, so lightly brush across the surface.
- To remove blood, scribble over stain with a cake of bathroom soap dipped in cold water as though using a crayon. For a large area, have a glass of water with you to dip as you go.
- Scrub over the stain with an old toothbrush in every direction – north, south, east and west.

■ Remove excess soap by wiping with a cold, damp cloth. Polish the soap off as though polishing a table. Wipe from the centre of the stain outwards.

■ Absorb moisture by covering the area with paper towel and standing on it. Continue to change the paper towel until it's no longer wet when you stand on it.

On cotton/non-upholstery fabric

■ Quickly pour a large quantity of cold water through the stain.

■ Scrub with a cake of bathroom soap and rub the fabric against itself using your hands.

■ If there's a shadow mark, wipe with glycerine, leave for 90 minutes, then rub with a cake of bathroom soap. If needed, repeat.

■ If the stain has set, wipe with 2 drops of glycerine and leave for several hours in a cool, dry place.

■ In all cases, wash according to the fabric. Dry on the clothesline or clothes airer. For silk and wool, gently wring and dry flat on a towel in the shade. Ensure silk is dried away from the wind so the fibres don't tangle and leave a dusty look.

On a mattress

■ For a fresh stain, scribble with a cake of bathroom soap dipped in cold water as though using a crayon.

■ Wipe with a damp cloth.

■ Leave to dry. Repeat, if needed.

- For an old stain, mix equal parts cornflour, glycerine and water to the consistency of thickened cream.
- Leave on the stain until it dries.
- Sprinkle with non-iodised salt.
- Brush off with a stiff brush.
- You may need to repeat these steps a few times for an old mattress because old stains can be particularly difficult to remove.

BOOTS

(see SHOES)

BOWLS

To clean

- Rinse in the sink before washing with a little dishwashing liquid and warm water.
- Rinse with fresh, clean water to remove soap residue.
- Alternatively, wipe with a small amount of salt and water. The salt acts as a mild abrasive.
- Rinse with clean water and allow to dry. The bowl must dry completely or it will quickly go mouldy.

CAR INTERIOR

For specific stains, consult the relevant section.

To clean inside the car

- Vacuum.
- Mix ½ teaspoon of dishwashing liquid in 1 litre of water until it froths.
- Wipe using the froth only on a cloth.
- Wipe off with a damp cloth.
- When dry, vacuum. Wipe over hard surfaces with lemon juice to remove the smell.

To remove dog vomit

- Remove excess by lifting the solids with a plastic comb or blotting liquids with paper towel.
- Scribble with a cake of bathroom soap dipped in cold water as though using a crayon.
- Place 2 drops of dishwashing liquid on your fingertips and massage into the stain with your fingers. Close your eyes so you can feel when the texture becomes like jelly. Wipe with a damp cloth until the dishwashing liquid is removed.
- If the vomit is a caramel colour, lightly wipe across the surface with 2 drops of glycerine on an old toothbrush. Leave for 90 minutes. Dip a cake of bathroom soap in cold water and scribble on the stain as though using a crayon. Fold a damp cloth flat and polish the stain out.
- In all cases, absorb moisture by covering the area with paper towel and standing or pressing on it. Continue to change the paper towel until it's no longer wet when you stand or press on it. When almost dry, repeat.

- If a shadow mark appears after a couple of weeks, repeat the process.
- If there's a watermark, place 1 cup of unprocessed wheat bran in a large bowl. Add drops of white vinegar one at a time, stirring as you go, until the mixture resembles breadcrumbs. It shouldn't be wet. Place the mixture into the toe of pantyhose and tie up tightly. It will be the size of a tennis ball. Rub over the stain. To remove the smell, mix 1 tablespoon of lemon juice with 1 litre of water in a spray pack and mist over the area.

CARPET

Flooded with water

- Hire a steam cleaner at the supermarket that comes with a bottle of carpet cleaning chemicals.
- Use half the amount of the carpet cleaning chemicals and top up with 2 tablespoons of bicarb, 2 tablespoons of white vinegar, 2 tablespoons of methylated spirits, 2 teaspoons of glycerine and 2 teaspoons of eucalyptus oil.
- Run the steam cleaner over the entire area of carpet.
- Repeat on empty until moisture is drawn out.

CAT LITTER TRAY/BOX

(see KITTY LITTER TRAY/BOX)

COLLAR/LEAD/HARNESS

To clean

- If made of nylon or polycotton, wet with dishwashing liquid and warm water.
- Standing over the sink, wrap the collar, lead or harness around a pen in a spiral pattern and hold the end with a thumb. Release your thumb and pull the other end. As the item twists around the pencil, the dirt and water will flick off. Repeat until all the water is removed.
- If made of leather, rub with saddle soap and pantyhose until clean. Remove excess saddle soap by wiping over the collar with damp pantyhose. Dry in the shade so the collar doesn't go stiff.
- If it has metal-backed studs, dry quickly because the metal can rust. Saliva can cause buckles to rust so clean as soon as possible.

DANDER

Dander is microscopic dead skin particles that collect in an animal's coat and are a major cause of allergic reactions.

On carpet/upholstery

- If there's a greasy mark, put 1 cup of unprocessed wheat bran in a bowl and add drops of white vinegar until the mixture resembles breadcrumbs. It shouldn't feel wet. Place the mixture into the toe of a pair of pantyhose and tie it up tightly. It should be the size of a tennis ball. Trim the excess pantyhose. Lightly mist the surface with water from a spray pack (on the mist setting) or lightly wipe with a cloth that is damp, not wet. Brush the pantyhose across the dirty surface like a big eraser.

- On carpet, sweep over the area with unprocessed wheat bran then vacuum.

DIARRHOEA

(see also POO)

On carpet/upholstery

- Remove excess by lifting the solids with a plastic comb or blotting liquids with paper towel.
- Create an edge around the stain with either talcum powder or paper towel.
- Scribble over the stained area with a cake of bathroom soap dipped in cold water as though using a crayon. Work from the outside to the inside of the stain.
- Wipe with damp pantyhose rolled into a ball.
- If any stain remains, place 2 drops of dishwashing liquid on your fingertips and massage into the stain with your fingers. Close your eyes so you can feel when the texture becomes like jelly.
- Wipe with a damp cloth until the dishwashing liquid is removed.

- Absorb moisture by covering the area with paper towel and standing on it. Continue to change the paper towel until it's no longer wet when you stand or press on it.

On non-upholstery fabric

- Remove excess under the tap using cold water.
- Scribble with a cake of bathroom soap run under cold water as though using a crayon.
- If a stain remains, massage with a couple of drops of dishwashing liquid on your fingertips until the liquid feels like jelly.
- Rinse using cold water.
- Alternatively, mix ½ lid of Vanish NapiSan Oxi Action in a 9-litre bucket of cold water and soak for 20 minutes. (Don't use Vanish NapiSan Oxi Action on wool, silk or leather.)
- Alternatively, soak overnight in a bucket of cold water with ¼ cup of bicarb.
- In all cases, wash according to the fabric. Dry in sunshine.

DIRT

On cotton/other fabric (not wool, silk or leather)

- Remove excess under the tap using cold water.
- Mix Vanish NapiSan Oxi Action and blood-heat (body temperature) to hot water to the consistency of spreadable butter. (Don't use Vanish NapiSan Oxi Action on wool, silk or leather.)

- Apply to the stain and leave for 20 minutes.
- Wash according to the fabric. Dry on the clothesline or a clothes airer.

On leather

- Wipe with saddle soap on a damp cloth.
- Polish with a clean cloth.
- Wipe with leather conditioner. Make your own by placing 1 teaspoon of beeswax, 1 teaspoon of lavender oil and 1 teaspoon of lemon oil on a 100 per cent cotton cloth, such as an old T-shirt. Place in the microwave in a microwave-safe dish. Microwave on high in 10-second bursts until the beeswax melts. After using the cloth, place it in a zip-lock bag and store in the freezer ready to use again.
- For kid leather, mix unprocessed wheat bran and drops of white vinegar until the mixture resembles breadcrumbs. Either place the mixture in the toe of pantyhose and wipe over the kid leather or apply directly.
- If your dog has rolled in decomposing soil in which animals have died, wash with dog shampoo then in warm water with a cake of bathroom soap.

DOG COAT OIL

On fabric

- Place 1 cup of unprocessed wheat bran in a large bowl. Add drops of white vinegar one at a time, stirring as you go, until the mixture resembles breadcrumbs. It shouldn't be wet. Add ½ teaspoon of dishwashing liquid to the mixture.

- Place the mixture into the toe of pantyhose and tie up tightly. It will be the size of a tennis ball.
- Lightly mist the surface with water from a spray pack (on the mist setting) or lightly wipe with a cloth that is damp, not wet.
- Brush the pantyhose ball across the dirty surface.
- When the stain is removed, spray with hairspray to protect it.

DROOL

(see SALIVA)

FAECES

(see POO)

FISH TANK

To clean a tank over 40 litres (weekly)

- Keep the fish and contents in the tank.
- If there's algae, wipe over the inside of the glass with pantyhose wrapped over your hand like a mitt. Do this before removing the water.
- Remove 15 per cent of the water.
- Clean 25 per cent of the gravel with a siphon. Or remove 25 per cent of the gravel, place it in a sieve and flush with boiling water. Allow to dry.

- If you have to clean the filter, don't change all the water at the same time. Rinse new filters under cold running water.
- Replace the water. Match the water temperature by filling a plastic bag with fresh water, sit the bag in the existing tank water until the water inside the plastic bag is the same temperature as the water in the tank, then slowly add the new water to the tank water. If it's a large amount of water, transfer it from a bucket (uncontaminated with detergents) using a siphon. Leave a gap between the top of the water and the top of the tank for oxygen exchange.
- Wipe the outside of the tank with white vinegar on a cloth. Never use strong detergents because they can seep into the water and harm your fish.

To clean a tank over 40 litres (quarterly)

- Unplug the heater.
- Remove plants and decorations and wipe the inside of the glass with pantyhose – wrap the pantyhose over your hand to create a mitt.
- Using a fish net, transfer fish to a large clean glass bowl. Add water scooped from the fish tank to lessen the shock to the fish – don't leave them here for more than 30 minutes. Put 1 or 2 plants or decorations from the tank into the bowl.
- Siphon at least 25 per cent and no more than 50 per cent of the water into a bucket designated for the task so there's no contamination from detergent residue. Never use soap, detergents or old kitchen sponges when cleaning a fish tank because the residue is harmful to fish.

- Remove the filter and clean it in the sink.
- Clean the gravel with a gravel cleaner or place in a sieve and flush with boiling water. Allow to dry.
- Match the water temperature by filling a plastic bag with fresh water, sit the bag in the existing tank water until the water inside the plastic bag is the same temperature as the water in the tank, then slowly add the new water to the tank water. Refill the tank.
- Replace plants and ornaments and reconnect the filter.
- Add salt or conditioner.
- Plug in the heater and restart the pump.
- Return the fish.
- Wipe the outside of the tank with white vinegar on a cloth. Never use strong detergents because they can seep into the water and harm your fish.

FLEAS

Fleas don't like mint, particularly pennyroyal and Persian mint.

To deter

- If there's a pregnant woman or pet in the house, use Persian mint, which is available as a low-growing plant in nurseries. Crush 1 tablespoon of fresh Persian mint leaves in a mortar and pestle and steep them in 1 tablespoon of methylated spirits and 1 litre of boiling water. Strain the mixture and lightly spray every 9 days.

- Alternatively, mix ¼ teaspoon of oil of pennyroyal in 1 litre of water. Every 9 days, lightly spray over a flea-infested area. Put on a pair of disposable rubber gloves and place 2 drops of oil of pennyroyal in the palm of your hand. Rub your hands together and pat the pet from head to tail. If they're reluctant, wait until they're sleeping and place a drop on the back of their neck between their shoulder blades.

⚠ WARNING

Don't use oil of pennyroyal if anyone, including your pet, is pregnant.

- Alternatively, wash with cold mint tea. To create this mix, add 2 teaspoons of dried mint or 4 teaspoons of fresh mint to 240 ml of hot water. Steep the tea for 15 minutes and strain. Allow it to cool. Then add it to the wash water. Or use mint sauce.

FLOODING

(see WATER FLOODING)

FUR

(see HAIR)

FUR BALL

Fur balls often leave a red–brown stain.

To clean

- Lightly wipe the surface with 2 drops of glycerine and leave for 24 hours.
- Scribble with a cake of bathroom soap dipped in cold water as if using a crayon.
- Wipe with a damp cloth.
- Absorb moisture by covering the area with paper towel and standing on it. Continue to change the paper towel until it's no longer wet when you stand on it.

GRASS

On carpet/upholstery

- Remove excess by vacuuming.
- Wipe with white spirits on a cloth.
- Sprinkle with talcum powder.
- When dry, vacuum again.
- Place white vinegar on a cloth and wring tightly so it's damp but not wet. Blot over the mark.
- Absorb moisture by covering the area with paper towel and standing on it. Continue to change the paper towel until it's no longer wet when you stand on it.

On cotton/other fabric

- Remove excess under the tap using cold water.
- Blot with or soak in white spirits.
- Wash according to the fabric.
- Dry on the clothesline or a clothes airer.

HAIR

On carpet

- Place a condom over the bristles of a soft broom and wash with a cake of bathroom soap and water.
- Sweep over the carpet. The hair will stick to the condom.
- Keep a bucket filled with water to rinse as you go.
- Vacuum.

On fabric/upholstery

- Put on a pair of disposable rubber gloves and wash your gloved hands with a cake of bathroom soap and water. Shake your hands dry.
- Wipe over the hair. It will stick to the gloves.

On hard surfaces

- Vacuum.
- Scatter a little unprocessed wheat bran over the surface and sweep. The bran will stick to the hair.
- Vacuum.

HARNESS

(see COLLAR/LEAD/HARNESS)

HUTCH

To clean

- Remove the contents of the hutch including uneaten food.
- Sweep the floor with a brush or broom and wipe surfaces with a damp cloth.
- To remove urine stains, wipe with white vinegar on a cloth.
- If the hutch is outside, clean using a hose. If it has a wire base over lawn, keep moving it to different areas and hose over the old area to break down faeces and residue.
- To deter bugs, wipe the interior with 2 drops of lemon oil and 5 drops of lavender oil on a cloth.
- After cleaning, place newspaper or straw at the bottom of the hutch, with recycled paper on top.

ICE CREAM

Dogs love to eat ice cream but it can be tricky to remove.

On carpet/upholstery

- Remove excess by blotting with paper towel.
- Scribble with a cake of bathroom soap run under cold water as though using a crayon.

- Scrub with an old toothbrush in all directions – north, south, east and west.
- Place 2 drops of dishwashing liquid on your fingertips and massage into the stain with your fingers. Close your eyes so you can feel when the texture becomes like jelly.
- Wipe with a damp cloth.
- Tightly wring a cloth in white vinegar so it's damp but not wet. Blot over the mark.
- Place the vinegar cloth in one hand and a dry cloth in the other and wipe hand over hand, as though stroking a cat, until the stain is removed.
- Absorb moisture by covering the area with paper towel and standing on it. Continue to change the paper towel until it's no longer wet when you stand on it.

On cotton/other fabric (not wool)

- Remove excess under the tap using cold water.
- Scribble with a cake of bathroom soap run under cold water.
- Place 2 drops of dishwashing liquid on your fingertips and massage into the stain with your fingers. Close your eyes so you can feel when the texture becomes like jelly.
- Rinse in blood-heat (body temperature) water.
- Blot with or soak in white vinegar until the stain is removed.
- Wash according to the fabric. Dry on the clothesline or a clothes airer.

KENNEL

To clean

- Remove the contents of the kennel and wipe the interior with white vinegar on a cloth.
- Wipe with a cake of bathroom soap and cold water on a cloth.
- To remove the smell, mix ¼ teaspoon of oil of cloves, 2 tablespoons of dried mint and 1 litre of hot water in a spray pack. Allow to cool. Spray over every surface and wipe with pantyhose. Reapply once a month.
- For portable kennels made of powder-coated steel and polyester fabric, wash the fabric with a cake of bathroom soap and cold water.

KITTY LITTER TRAY/BOX

To clean

- Wash the tray or box with hot soapy water.
- If the kitty litter smells, empty the box or tray and pour 5 mm of white vinegar inside. Let it stand for 20 minutes and rinse with cold water.

LEAD

(see COLLAR/LEAD/HARNESS)

LITTER TRAY/BOX

(see KITTY LITTER TRAY/BOX)

MANURE

(see POO)

MOULD

On glass

- Mix ¼ teaspoon of oil of cloves and 1 litre of water in a spray pack.
- Spray mixture onto a cloth.
- Wipe the glass with the cloth.

On timber

- Mix ¼ teaspoon of oil of cloves in a 1-litre spray pack of water.
- Spray onto a broom head and wipe over the mould.
- Leave for 24 hours and repeat.

MYSTERY STAINS – PET AND NON-PET RELATED

If you don't know what the stain is, use this guide.

Proteins

- These have a dark ring around the edge and include blood and meat.
- To remove, use cold water and scribble with a cake of bathroom soap as if using a crayon. On fabrics, rub the fabric against itself to loosen the stain. Don't use blood-heat (body temperature) or hot water, or you'll set the stain.

Carbohydrates

- These stains are darker in the centre and lighter around the edge and feel stiff. The sources include **sugary foods** and **starches**.
- To remove **sugar stains**, use blood-heat (body temperature) water and scribble with a cake of bathroom soap as though using a crayon. Rub the fabric against itself to loosen the stain.
- To remove **starchy stains**, use cold water and scribble with a cake of bathroom soap as though using a crayon. Rub the fabric against itself to loosen the stain. If in doubt, use cold water first.

Fats/oils

- Fat and oil stains spread evenly across a surface, feel greasy between your fingers and, if you wash the stained garment, continue to spread.
- To remove **lighter oils**, massage with dishwashing liquid on your fingertips until the liquid feels like jelly. This means the oil has been emulsified and is water-soluble. Wipe with a damp cloth or rinse under blood-heat water.

- For **darker or thicker oils**, such as engine grease, use baby oil to dilute the stain before following the instructions above.

Pigments

- These include **ink**, **paint**, **dye**, **rust** and **oxide**, and each requires a different solution.
- For **ink** stains, leave full-cream milk in the sun to rot and place rotten milk solids over the stain. The ink will be absorbed into the solids. Alternatively, rub with white spirits on a cotton bud.
- Permanent pen markers contain their own solvent, so write over the mark with the same pen, and while it's wet, wipe with white spirits on a cotton bud.
- For children's or artists' watercolour **paint**, blot with water on a cloth until removed.
- For water-based paint, use methylated spirits on a cotton bud or cotton ball.
- For oil-based paint, use white spirits or turpentine on a cotton bud or cotton ball.
- For fresh vinyl-based paint, blot with a couple of drops of dishwashing liquid on a damp, cold cloth.
- For old vinyl-based paint, blot with methylated spirits on a cloth.
- To remove **rust** from hard surfaces, use proprietary products CLR or Ranex and always wear disposable rubber gloves when using. Don't get CLR or Ranex on your skin because it can cause irritation.

- To remove rust from absorbent surfaces, use lemon juice and salt.
- For an **oxide** stain, wipe with 2 drops of glycerine on a cloth and remove any remaining colour by exposing the stain to ultraviolet light. Protect the area around the ultraviolet light with cardboard.

Resins

- These feel sticky to the touch.
- For plant-based resins such as tree sap, wipe with glycerine or tea tree oil.
- The solvent for shellac is methylated spirits applied with a cloth.
- For superglue, remove with superglue remover or acetone.
- For craft and PVA glues (which go on white and dry clear), use steam.
- For 2-part epoxy glues (e.g. Araldite), remove with acetone.

OINTMENT

Prescription ointment contains different chemical compositions. This advice is for non-prescription ointment.

On carpet/upholstery

- Remove excess by lifting with a plastic comb or blotting with paper towel.
- For water-based ointment, scribble with a cake of bathroom soap run under blood-heat (body temperature) water as

though using a crayon. Massage with your fingertips until the stain is loosened. Wipe with a damp cloth. Repeat, if needed.

- For grey staining, massage with 2 drops of dishwashing liquid on your fingertips until the liquid feels like jelly. Wipe with a damp cloth until the dishwashing liquid is removed.
- For antibacterial ointment, combine 1 teaspoon of soap flakes or grated bathroom soap, 1 teaspoon of dishwashing liquid and 1 tablespoon of boiling water, and mix until the soap dissolves. Massage 2 drops of the solution into the stain using your fingertips until the solution feels like jelly. Place a cold, damp cloth in one hand and a dry cloth in the other and wipe hand over hand, as though stroking a cat, until the stain is removed.
- For wax-based ointment, mix 2 drops of tea tree oil and 2 drops of dishwashing liquid and massage with your fingertips until the liquid feels like jelly. Wipe with a cold, damp cloth. Repeat, if needed.
- For liniment (alcohol-based), wring a cloth in white vinegar, place over the stain and stand on it for 5 seconds. Remove.
- In all cases, absorb moisture by covering the area with paper towel and standing on it. Continue to change the paper towel until it's no longer wet when you stand on it.

On cotton/other fabric (not wool)

- Remove excess under the tap using blood-heat (body temperature) water.

- For water-based ointment, scribble with a cake of bathroom soap as though using a crayon. Massage with your fingertips until the stain is loosened.
- For grey staining, massage with a couple of drops of dishwashing liquid on your fingertips until the liquid feels like jelly.
- For antibacterial ointment, combine 1 teaspoon of soap flakes or grated bathroom soap, 1 teaspoon of dishwashing liquid and 1 tablespoon of boiling water. Allow the mixture to dissolve. Massage 2 drops of the solution into the stain with your fingertips until the solution feels like jelly.
- For wax-based ointment, mix 2 drops of tea tree oil with 2 drops of dishwashing liquid and massage with your fingertips until the liquid feels like jelly.
- For liniment (alcohol-based), blot with or soak in white vinegar.
- In all cases, wash according to the fabric. Dry on the clothesline or a clothes airer.

PEE

(see URINE)

PET LOO

To clean

- Spray with white vinegar and water and wipe with a cloth.
- Rinse with fresh water.

PETROLEUM JELLY (VASELINE)

On carpet/upholstery

- Remove excess by lifting with a plastic comb or blotting with paper towel.
- Place 2 drops of dishwashing liquid on your fingertips and massage into the stain with your fingers. Close your eyes so you can feel when the texture becomes like jelly.
- Wipe with a damp cloth until dishwashing liquid is removed.
- Absorb moisture by covering the area with paper towel and standing on it. Continue to change the paper towel until it's no longer wet when you stand on it.

On cotton/other fabric (not wool)

- Remove excess by blotting with a cloth.
- Place 2 drops of dishwashing liquid on your fingertips and massage into the stain with your fingers. Close your eyes so you can feel when the texture becomes like jelly.
- Wash according to the fabric. Dry on the clothesline or a clothes airer.

On wool

- Massage with 1 teaspoon of cheap shampoo using your fingertips.
- Rinse in 1 teaspoon of cheap hair conditioner and blood-heat (body temperature) water.
- Rinse under blood-heat water.
- Gently wring and dry flat on a towel in the shade.

POO

(see also BIRD POO)

Poo is high in protein and fat.

On carpet/upholstery

- Remove excess by lifting the solids with a plastic comb or blotting liquids with paper towel.
- Scribble with a cake of bathroom soap run under cold water as though using a crayon. If stubborn, scrub with an old toothbrush or pantyhose.
- Leave to dry.
- Vacuum.
- Alternatively, remove excess then fill a bucket with cold water and enough dishwashing liquid to generate a sudsy mix. Use your hands or a brush to create suds.
- Apply only the suds with an old toothbrush, using as little water as possible, and work in all directions – north, south, east and west.
- Absorb moisture by covering the area with paper towel and standing on it. Continue to change the paper towel until it's no longer wet when you stand on it.

For caramel colouring on carpet/upholstery

- Lightly brush across the surface with 2 drops of glycerine on an old toothbrush (use 2 drops of glycerine for every 30 cm of stained area). Don't push into carpet or fabric backing or you will release tannin stains. Leave for 90 minutes.

- Dip a cake of bathroom soap in cold water and scribble over the stain as you would with a crayon.
- Fold a damp cloth flat and polish the stain out.
- Absorb moisture by covering the area with paper towel and standing on it. Continue to change the paper towel until it's no longer wet when you stand on it.

For orange-coloured poo on carpet/ upholstery

- Pumpkin can be added to animals' food to firm their stools, but it means the poo becomes very orange in colour.
- Tightly wring a cloth in white vinegar so it's damp but not wet. Blot over the mark.
- Expose to sunlight or ultraviolet light. If using ultraviolet light, protect areas around the stain with cardboard. Check every 2 hours.
- Absorb moisture by covering the area with paper towel and standing on it. Continue to change the paper towel until it's no longer wet when you stand on it.

On leather shoes

- Place the shoes in sunshine and allow the poo to dry out.
- Using a shoe brush, remove as much poo as you can. Then wipe with leather conditioner. Make your own by placing 1 teaspoon of beeswax, 1 teaspoon of lavender oil and 1 teaspoon of lemon oil on a 100 per cent cotton cloth, such as an old T-shirt. Place in the microwave in a microwave-safe dish. Microwave on high in 10-second bursts until the

beeswax melts. After using the cloth, place it in a zip-lock bag and store in the freezer ready to use again.

- If the poo has penetrated through the leather, wipe with cheap shampoo and blood-heat (body temperature) water on a cloth and flush in blood-heat water. Dry slowly in the shade with newspaper inside the shoes to hold their shape. Wipe with leather conditioner to create a protective surface.

On timber walls

- Dry the timber in sunshine or with a hair dryer. Remove as much poo as possible.
- Coat the bristles of a stiff brush using a cake of bathroom soap and cold water and scrub over stains. Allow to dry.
- If stains remain, mix plaster of Paris and water to the consistency of peanut butter. Add 1 teaspoon of glycerine per cup of mixture and paint over the stain with a brush. Allow to dry completely. If it feels cold on the back of your hand, it's not dry.
- When dry, crack it with the back of the brush and sweep away.

SADDLE

For leather

- Roll a pair of pantyhose into a ball the size of a mandarin.
- Dampen it with water and wipe over the saddle.
- Use the pantyhose to apply saddle soap and rub it over the leather.

- When there's no more drag on the leather, remove soap using paper towel or a dry clean cloth.
- To prevent colour transfer to your riding clothes, seal the leather by wiping with leather conditioner on a cloth. Make your own by placing 1 teaspoon of beeswax, 1 teaspoon of lavender oil and 1 teaspoon of lemon oil on a cotton cloth, such as an old T-shirt. Place in the microwave in a microwave-safe dish. Microwave on high in 10-second bursts until the beeswax melts. After using the cloth, place it in a zip-lock bag and store in the freezer ready to use again.

For synthetics

- Rinse with dishwashing liquid and cold water. Dry thoroughly.

SALIVA

For cat saliva

- Cat saliva has an organic deposit in which bacteria can grow. Mix 1 teaspoon of lavender oil per 1 litre of water in a spray pack. Spray over the saliva and wipe with a cloth.

On car exterior

- Wash with a cake of bathroom soap and water.
- Polish with a cutting compound. Make your own by mixing equal parts glycerine and talcum powder and apply with tightly rolled pantyhose. To speed up the task, apply using a sheepskin buff.

On carpet/upholstery

- Hire a steam cleaner at the supermarket that comes with a bottle of carpet cleaning chemicals.
- Use half the amount of carpet cleaning chemicals and top up with 2 tablespoons of bicarb, 2 tablespoons of white vinegar, 2 tablespoons of methylated spirits, 2 teaspoons of glycerine and 2 teaspoons of eucalyptus oil.
- Use the upholstery arm of the cleaner and steam clean the entire panel, not just the stained area.
- Repeat on empty to draw out moisture.

On glass

- As soon as you spot saliva, wash it with soapy water.
- If the glass is permanently etched, wipe with white vinegar then rub with sweet almond oil and reapply as needed.

On leather

- For plasticised leather, wipe with white vinegar on a cloth. Then wipe with leather conditioner. Make your own by placing 1 teaspoon of beeswax, 1 teaspoon of lavender oil and 1 teaspoon of lemon oil on a 100 per cent cotton cloth, such as an old T-shirt. Place in the microwave in a microwave-safe dish. Microwave on high in 10-second bursts until the beeswax melts. After using the cloth, place it in a zip-lock bag and store in the freezer ready to use again.

■ For tanned leather (school shoes, bags), wipe with white spirits in even, parallel strokes over the entire panel, sprinkle with talcum powder and leave to dry. When dry, brush off the talcum powder. Don't remove before it's dry or the leather will resemble mange.

■ For soft leather, wash the entire panel with equal parts white vinegar and water. Leave to dry slowly in the shade then wipe with leather conditioner. Make your own – see instructions on previous page. For wearable items, such as jackets, wear until the vinegar and water dry to help stop the leather going stiff.

■ For leather on cotton and parachute fibre collars and leads, wash in the washing machine.

SATIN

To clean

■ Remove solid matter by sprinkling with talcum powder and drying with a hair dryer. Move in the direction of the grain.

■ Hand wash in 1 teaspoon of cheap hair shampoo and 9 litres of cold water. Soak for 5 minutes and rinse thoroughly under cold water.

■ Don't wring satin but remove water by rolling the item in a clean towel. Apply pressure as you roll. Lay flat in the shade on a clean towel to dry.

■ Iron on a medium heat.

SCRATCH MARKS

On leather

- For brown leather, cut a walnut (the nut, not the shell) in half and rub one of the cut surfaces over the scratch. Leave for 1 hour for the colour to cure.
- For other leather, use shoe cream (not shoe polish or wax) that matches the colour of the leather. Apply with a cloth over the scratched area only.
- Rub the scratches with the back of a hot stainless-steel spoon (dip the spoon in a glass of boiling water and dry with a tea towel) to set the shoe cream.
- Wipe with leather conditioner. Make your own by placing 1 teaspoon of beeswax, 1 teaspoon of lavender oil and 1 teaspoon of lemon oil on a 100 per cent cotton cloth, such as an old T-shirt. Place in the microwave in a microwave-safe dish. Microwave on high in 10-second bursts until the beeswax melts. After using the cloth, place it in a zip-lock bag and store in the freezer ready to use again.

On plastic

- Wipe with equal parts glycerine and talcum powder on a cloth.

On polyurethane

- Polish with 2 drops of Brasso on a rolled-up pair of pantyhose using speed rather than pressure. It will look worse before it looks better. The Brasso partially melts the polyurethane. Only use a small amount of Brasso to avoid leaving a residue.

On stainless steel

- Wipe with a dab of Gumption on a cloth.
- Sprinkle with bicarb and spray with white vinegar.
- While fizzing, scrub with a damp cloth.
- Polish with rolled-up pantyhose.
- For deep scratches, apply jeweller's rouge with a felt buff or sheepskin buff on an electric drill.

On timber

- For unpolished timber, wipe with baby oil and black tea on a cloth.
- Alternatively, scribble with a crayon in a matching colour. Aim a hair dryer over the top to gently melt the crayon into the scratch and buff with rolled-up pantyhose.

On vinyl

- Mix equal parts glycerine and talcum powder to the consistency of spreadable butter.
- Polish on with tightly rolled pantyhose.
- Polish off with panthyhose.

SHOES

For rubber shoes/boots

- To keep rubber shoes or boots looking glossy, mix equal parts glycerine and sweet almond oil and wipe on with a cloth.

To remove smells

- Mix 2 tablespoons of bicarb, 2 tablespoons of talcum powder, 1 drop of tea tree oil, 1 drop of oil of cloves and 1 drop of lavender oil. For rubber shoes, add 2 tablespoons of unprocessed wheat bran and 1 teaspoon of salt.
- Place the mixture in the centre of a small piece of muslin or cotton voile and tie with string or ribbon. Alternatively, place inside a pair of pantyhose and tie up.
- Rub through the shoe.

SOIL

(see DIRT)

TICKS

'Freeze it, don't squeeze it' is the latest advice.

To remove

- Apply a spray that contains ether, such as Wart-Off or Medi Freeze Skin Tag Remover.
- Place the nozzle over the tick, spray and wait 10 minutes for the tick to die. Once it's dead, brush it off.[8]
- If in doubt, see your vet. If you live in a tick-prone area, medication is available from the vet.

---

8   www.abc.net.au/catalyst/stories/4177191.htm

TOOTHPASTE

Dogs love to eat toothpaste because of the minty flavour.
Remove toothpaste from surfaces as soon as possible because
it can bleach them.

On carpet/upholstery

- Remove excess by lifting with a plastic comb or blotting with
  paper towel.
- Tightly wring a cloth in white vinegar so it's damp but not
  wet. Blot over the mark.
- Absorb moisture by covering the area with paper towel and
  standing on it. Continue to change the paper towel until it's
  no longer wet when you stand on it.

On timber

- Wipe with water on rolled-up pantyhose.
- If the toothpaste has bleached the timber, wipe over the
  bleached area with a damp teabag. The tannins in tea draw
  out the tannins in the timber and replace the colour.

On wool

- Remove excess under the tap using blood-heat (body
  temperature) water.
- Blot with equal parts white vinegar and water on a cloth.
- Soak in 1 teaspoon of cheap shampoo and blood-heat water
  for 30 minutes.

- Rinse in blood-heat water.
- Gently wring and dry flat on a towel in the shade.

TOY

For a squeaky toy

- Mix ¼ teaspoon of tea tree oil and 1 litre of water in a spray pack. Tea tree oil is a great disinfectant and is non-toxic.
- Spray over the toy and wipe with a cloth.
- To clean a mouldy rubber toy, add ¼ teaspoon of oil of cloves to a 4-litre bucket of blood-heat (body temperature) water.
- Place the toy in the bucket, squeeze so water gets inside and leave for 2 hours.
- Remove, squeeze out the water and set aside to dry.

For a fabric toy

- Place inside a plastic bag and into the freezer to kill microscopic bugs and dust mites. This kills the mites but not the allergen that causes the allergic reaction.
- Check the label. Most soft toys can be washed in the washing machine on a gentle cycle. Instead of laundry detergent, use 1 tablespoon of cheap shampoo and 2 drops of tea tree oil to kill dust mites. Place in a delicates bag or pillowcase.
- Don't use the dryer but hang the toy to dry in sunshine.

- Alternatively, after removing from the freezer, add drops of white vinegar to 1 kg of unprocessed wheat bran until the mixture resembles breadcrumbs. Place inside a pillowcase and add the soft toy. Tie up and shake well.
- Remove the toy from the pillowcase and brush with a scrubbing brush.

URINE

You need to remove every bit of urine or the smell will linger. Many pets instinctively return to the same spot to urinate, so if pee isn't completely removed, the animal will pee there again.

On carpet/upholstery

- For fresh stains, remove excess by blotting with paper towel.
- Place white vinegar on a cloth and wring tightly so it's damp but not wet. Blot over the mark.
- For old stains, first find where the urine is. In a darkened room, turn on an ultraviolet light and the urine stains will show up yellow.
- Mark around the yellow stains with a piece of white chalk so you can identify the offending areas.
- Wipe inside the chalk marks with a cloth tightly wrung in white vinegar.
- Absorb moisture by covering the area with paper towel and standing on it. Continue to change the paper towel until it's no longer wet when you stand on it.

- If the urine has penetrated to the back of carpet, the jute releases a tannin stain. To fix this, place 2 drops of glycerine on an old toothbrush and lightly brush across the surface of the carpet. Be careful not to push the glycerine into the backing of the carpet or it will release more tannins. Leave for 90 minutes.
- Tightly wring a cloth in white vinegar. Hold it flat against the stained area and polish out as though polishing a table. Make sure you don't push your fingers into the carpet.
- Absorb moisture by covering the area with paper towel and standing on it. Continue to change the paper towel until it's no longer wet when you stand on it. If you need to clean again with glycerine and vinegar, wait 24 hours.

On stone (not marble or limestone)

- Wipe with white vinegar on a cloth.
- If stubborn, mix plaster of Paris and water to the consistency of peanut butter. To each cup of mixture, add 2 teaspoons of white vinegar.
- Spread 6 mm to 1.3 cm thick over the stain.
- Allow to dry completely. If it feels cold on the back of your hand, it's not dry.
- When dry, crack it with the back of a brush and sweep away.
- Don't use white vinegar on marble or limestone. Instead, add 1 teaspoon of soap flakes or grated bathroom soap to the plaster of Paris mix.

On timber

- For fresh stains, remove excess by blotting with paper towel.
- Place white vinegar on a cloth and wring tightly so it's damp but not wet. Blot over the mark.
- For old stains, first find where the urine is. In a darkened room, turn on an ultraviolet light and the urine stains will show up yellow.
- Mark around the yellow stains with a piece of white chalk so you can see where to clean.
- Wipe inside the chalk marks with a cloth tightly wrung in white vinegar.
- If the urine has soaked through the floorboard grooves, mix plaster of Paris and water to the consistency of peanut butter. For every cup of mixture, add 2 teaspoons of white vinegar.
- Spread 6 mm to 1.3 cm thick over the floorboards.
- Allow to dry completely. If it feels cold on the back of your hand, it's not dry.
- When dry, crack it with the back of a brush and remove.
- In the worst cases, where the urine has been there for years, you'll have to replace the floorboards.
- If the floors are coated in polyurethane and there are scratches, urine can penetrate through the scratches. To clean, mix 4 black teabags and ½ cup of white vinegar per bucket of hot water. Wipe this mixture over the surface with a cloth.

On unsealed terracotta

- Mix plaster of Paris and water to the consistency of peanut butter. For every cup of paste, add 2 tablespoons of white vinegar.
- In a darkened room, turn on an ultraviolet light and the urine stains will show up yellow.
- Mark around the yellow stains with a piece of white chalk so you can identify the offending areas.
- Paint the mixture over the stain 6 mm to 1.3 cm thick with a brush and leave for 24 hours.
- When completely dry, crack using the brush. If needed, repeat.
- To seal terracotta tiles, mix ½ cup of PVA glue in 1 cup of just-warm water. Sweep over the surface in even, parallel lines using a clean, soft kitchen broom.
- Leave to dry. Clean the broom immediately by massaging with dishwashing liquid and warm water.
- To remove the seal, scrub with a stiff broom and boiling water.

VASELINE

(see PETROLEUM JELLY [VASELINE])

VOMIT

On carpet/upholstery

- Remove excess by lifting solids with a plastic comb or blotting liquids with paper towel.

- Scribble with a cake of bathroom soap dipped in cold water as though using a crayon.
- Place 2 drops of dishwashing liquid on your fingertips and massage into the stain with your fingers. Close your eyes so you can feel when the texture becomes like jelly.
- Wipe with a damp cloth until the dishwashing liquid is removed.
- If the vomit is a caramel colour, lightly wipe with 2 drops of glycerine on an old toothbrush. Leave for 90 minutes. Wipe with a damp cloth. Dip a cake of bathroom soap in cold water and scribble over the stain as though using a crayon. Fold a damp cloth flat and polish the stain out.
- If there's a watermark, place 1 cup of unprocessed wheat bran in a large bowl. Add drops of white vinegar one at a time, stirring as you go, until the mixture resembles breadcrumbs. It shouldn't be wet. Place the mixture into the toe of pantyhose and tie up tightly. It will be the size of a tennis ball. Rub over the stain until removed.
- To remove stomach acids, lightly brush with 2 drops of glycerine on an old toothbrush. Leave for 90 minutes. Tightly wring a cloth in white vinegar. Hold it flat against the stained area and polish out as though polishing a table.
- To remove the smell, mix 1 tablespoon of lemon juice with 1 litre of water in a spray pack and spray over the area.
- In all cases, absorb moisture by covering the area with paper towel and standing on it. Continue to change the paper towel until it's no longer wet when you stand on it.

On cotton/other fabric

- Remove excess under the tap using cold water.
- Place 2 drops of dishwashing liquid on your fingertips and massage into the stain with your fingers. Close your eyes so you can feel when the texture becomes like jelly. Wipe with a damp cloth until the dishwashing liquid is removed.
- Blot with or soak in white vinegar (to remove bile, which contains hydrochloric acid).
- If there's residue, scrub with 2 drops of glycerine on an old toothbrush. Leave for 90 minutes. Blot with white vinegar and hang in sunshine until the stain fades before washing.
- Alternatively, soak in ½ lid of Vanish NapiSan Oxi Action and 9 litres of hot water for 30 minutes. Don't use on wool or silk. For wool and silk, rinse in 1 teaspoon of cheap shampoo and blood-heat (body temperature) water.
- Wash according to the fabric. Dry on the clothesline or a clothes airer.

On mattress

- Remove excess by lifting the solids with a plastic comb or blotting liquids with paper towel.
- Wash with a cake of bathroom soap or with dishwashing liquid. If there's a stain from caramel colouring, lightly wipe with 2 drops of glycerine on an old toothbrush. Leave for 90 minutes.
- Wipe with a damp cloth.
- To remove the smell, mix 1 tablespoon of lemon juice with 1 litre of water in a spray pack and spray over the mattress.

- If you can, put the mattress in the sun to dry it out and to kill bacteria.
- If you can't get it into the sunshine, dry with a hair dryer.

WATER FLOODING

On carpet

- Hire a steam cleaner from the supermarket that comes with carpet cleaning chemicals.
- Use only half the amount of carpet cleaning chemicals and top it up with 2 tablespoons of bicarb, 2 tablespoons of white vinegar, 2 tablespoons of methylated spirits, 4 teaspoons of glycerine and 2 teaspoons of eucalyptus oil.
- Work over the entire area of carpet.
- Repeat on empty until the moisture is drawn out.

CHAPTER 8

HOUSEHOLD
FORMULAS

BRAN BALL

(can be used on upholstery, fabric, suede)

- Put 1 cup of unprocessed wheat bran in a bowl and add white vinegar, one drop at a time, until the mixture resembles breadcrumbs – it should be clumping but not wet.
- Place the mixture into the toe of pantyhose and tie tightly. Rub the pantyhose across the surface of the fabric like an eraser.
- The bran ball can be reused again and again. Store in a zip-lock bag in the freezer. Add drops of white vinegar to re-moisten.

CARPET CLEANER

(for steam cleaning)

- Hire a steam cleaner at the supermarket that comes with carpet cleaning chemicals.
- Use half the amount of chemicals the manufacturer suggests and top up with 2 tablespoons of bicarb, 2 tablespoons of white vinegar, 2 tablespoons of methylated spirits, 2 teaspoons of glycerine and 2 teaspoons of eucalyptus oil.
- Leave any leftover solution in a 1-litre spray pack and use as needed. It's also a great multi-purpose spot cleaner.

FURNITURE POLISH/LEATHER CONDITIONER

- Place 1 teaspoon of beeswax, 1 teaspoon of lavender oil and 1 teaspoon of lemon oil on a 100 per cent cotton cloth, such as an old T-shirt.
- Place in the microwave in a microwave-safe dish. Microwave on high in 10-second bursts until the beeswax melts.
- When it cools, use it over leather and timber.
- After using the cloth, place it in a zip-lock bag and store in the freezer ready to use again.

GENERAL CLEANER FOR CARPET

- Mix 2 tablespoons of bicarb, 2 tablespoons of white vinegar, 2 tablespoons of methylated spirits, 2 teaspoons of glycerine, 2 teaspoons of eucalyptus oil, 2 teaspoons of dishwashing liquid and 1 litre of water in a spray pack. Lightly spray over carpet, then wipe carpet with a damp cloth.

GLYCERINE SOLUTION

(to remove tannin stains)
- Mix 2 tablespoons of glycerine with 2 cups of water in a 1-litre spray pack.
- Lightly mist over areas. Leave for 90 minutes. Wipe off with a damp cloth.

HARD SURFACE CLEANER

- Combine 1 teaspoon of lavender oil, 1 cup of white vinegar and 1 litre of water in a spray pack. Shake well before use.
- Lightly mist over hard surfaces, then wipe surfaces with a clean cloth.
- Don't use this on marble because white vinegar is an acid and will eat into the marble.

LAVENDER MIX

- Add 1 teaspoon of lavender oil to a 1-litre spray pack of water.

MINT TEA

- Add 2 teaspoons of dried mint or 4 teaspoons of fresh mint to 240 ml of hot water.
- Allow the tea to steep for 15 minutes and strain. Allow it to cool.
- Spray over surfaces, add to washing water, or use when washing your pet where fleas or flies are present.

SHOE FROU

- Mix 2 tablespoons of bicarb, 2 tablespoons of talcum powder, 1 drop of tea tree oil, 1 drop of oil of cloves, 1 drop of lavender oil, 2 tablespoons of unprocessed wheat bran and 1 teaspoon of salt.

- Place the mixture in the centre of a small piece of muslin or cotton voile and tie with string or ribbon. Alternatively, place inside a pair of pantyhose and tie up.
- Rub through the shoe. Store to use again.

SURFACE SEALANT: THE PIN TEST

Surfaces can be sealed with varnish, polyurethane, shellac or wax. To work out which sealant has been used, take a pin or needle, hold in a pair of pliers and heat on the stove. Touch the pin or needle to an inconspicuous part of the item and work out what smell it creates. If it smells like burnt plastic, it's coated in polyurethane. If it smells like an electrical fire, it's an oil-based varnish. If it smells like burnt hair, it's shellac. If it smells like a snuffed candle, it's wax.

To repair polyurethane, apply a little Brasso with a lint-free cloth and rub swiftly over the mark in the direction of the grain. It will look worse before it looks better. Brasso partially melts polyurethane and allows it to refill the tiny air holes that create white watermarks. Shellac, varnish and wax can be repaired using beeswax. Warm beeswax in a bowl in the microwave until it just softens and apply with the skin side of a piece of lemon peel. Rub in the direction of the grain using speed, not pressure.

QUICK GUIDE TO REMOVING STAINS FROM FABRIC

Apple – Wipe with 2 drops of glycerine on an old toothbrush and leave for 90 minutes. Wash normally.

Avocado – After removing excess, massage with 2 drops of dishwashing liquid on your fingers until the liquid feels like jelly. Wash normally.

Banana – Wipe with 2 drops of glycerine and leave for 90 minutes. Wash normally.

Blueberries – Blot with or soak in white vinegar. Wash normally. Hang in sunshine (UV fades stains).

Carbohydrates – Stains will be darker in the centre and lighter around the edge and will feel stiff. To remove sugar stains, use blood-heat (body temperature) water and scribble with a cake of bathroom soap as you would with a crayon. Rub the fabric against itself to loosen the stain. Wash according to the fabric. To remove starchy stains, use cold water and scribble with a cake of bathroom soap as you would with a crayon. Rub the fabric against itself to loosen the stain. Wash according to the fabric. If in doubt, use cold water first.

Carrot – Blot with or soak in white vinegar. Wash normally. Hang in sunshine (UV fades stains).

Cereal – Scribble with a cake of bathroom soap as if using a crayon and rinse in blood-heat (body temperature) water. Wash normally.

Egg – Scribble with a cake of bathroom soap as if using a crayon and rinse in blood-heat (body temperature) water. Wash normally.

Fats/oils – These spread evenly across a surface, feel greasy between your fingers and, if you wash the stained garment, continue to spread. To remove cooking oils, massage with dishwashing liquid on your fingertips until the liquid feels like jelly. This means the oil has been emulsified and is water-soluble. Wipe with a damp cloth.

Milk – Rinse with cold water and a cake of bathroom soap and wash normally.

Pear – Wipe with 2 drops of glycerine and leave for 90 minutes. Wash normally.

Peas – Blot with or soak in white vinegar. Wash normally.

Proteins – Stains have a dark ring around the edge and include blood, seeds, nuts, meat, cheese, milk, other dairy and fish. To remove, use cold water and scribble with a cake of bathroom soap as though using a crayon. Rub the fabric against itself to loosen the stain. Wash according to the fabric. Don't use blood-heat (body temperature) or hot water, or you'll set the stain.

Pumpkin – Blot with or soak in white vinegar. Wash normally. Hang in sunshine (UV fades stains).

Sunscreen – Massage with 2 drops of dishwashing liquid on your fingertips, then wash with warm water.

Sweet potato – Scribble with a cake of bathroom soap as though using a crayon. Wash normally.

Tomato puree – Blot with or soak in white vinegar. Wash normally. Hang in sunshine (UV fades stains).

Watermelon – This becomes alcoholic very quickly, causing a smell. Sponge with white vinegar and sprinkle with bicarb to remove the stain and the smell.

APPENDIX 2

IDEAL DOG WEIGHTS

Dogs in a healthy weight range live longer than overweight ones. Here's a list of ideal weights according to breed and sex.[9]

9   www.vetwest.com.au/pet-library/weight-the-ideal-bodyweight-range-for-
    your-dog-by-breed

Breed	Dogs (kg)	Bitches (kg)
Affenpinscher	3-4	3-4
Afghan Hound	27-32	23-30
Airedale Terrier	20-23	20-23
Akita	38.6-49.9	38.6-49.9
Alaskan Malamute	38-56	38-56
Australian Cattle Dog	20-22	20-22
Australian Kelpie	20.5-25	18-27
Australian Silky Terrier	3.5-4.5	3.5-4.5
Australian Terrier	6.5	6.5
Basenji	11	9.5
Basset Hound	18-27	16-23
Beagle	13-16	11-13
Bearded Collie	20.5-25	18-27
Bedlington Terrier	8.25-10.4	8.25-10.4
Bichon Frise	8-9	7-8
Bloodhound	41-50	36-45
Border Collie	19-24	18-22
Border Terrier	5.9-7.1	5.1-6.4
Borzoi	32-39	23-32
Boston Terrier	4.5-11	4.5-11
Bouvier des Flandres	35-40	27-35
Boxer	30-32	25-27
Briard	36-41	32-36

Breed	Dogs (kg)	Bitches (kg)
British Bulldog	25	22.7
Brittany Spaniel	15	13
Bull Mastiff	50–59	41–50
Bull Terrier	18–23	18–23
Bull Terrier (Miniature)	9	9
Cavalier King Charles Spaniel	5.4–8.1	5.4–8.1
Chesapeake Bay Retriever	36	29.5
Chihuahua	2.7	2.7
Chinese Crested Dog	5–5.5	5–5.5
Chow Chow	23–32	18–32
Collie	20.5–29.5	18–25
Dachshund	9–12	9–12
Dachshund (Miniature)	4.5	4.5
Dalmation	27	25
Dandie Dinmont Terrier	8–11	8–11
Deerhound	45.5	36.5
Doberman	34–41	29.5–36
Elkhound	23	20
English Toy Terrier (Black & Tan)	2.7–3.6	2.7–3.6
Finnish Spitz	14–16	14–16
Fox Terrier (Smooth)	7.25–8.25	6.75–7.75
Fox Terrier (Wire)	8.25	8.25
Foxhound	32	32

Breed	Dogs (kg)	Bitches (kg)
French Bulldog	12.7	10.9
German Shepherd	34–38.5	27–32
German Shorthaired Pointer	25–32	20–27
German Wirehaired Pointer	25–34	20.5–29
Great Dane	min. 54	min. 46
Greyhound	30–32	27–30
Griffon Bruxellois	2.2–4.9	2.2–4.9
Hungarian Puli	13–15	10–13
Hungarian Vizsla	20–30	20–30
Irish Terrier	12.2	11.3
Irish Wolfhound	54.5	40.9
Italian Greyhound	2.7–4.5	2.7–4.5
Japanese Chin	1.8–3.2	1.8–3.2
Keeshond	16–23	16–20.5
Kerry Blue Terrier	15–17	16
King Charles Spaniel	3.6–6.3	3.6–6.3
Lakeland Terrier	7.7	6.8
Large Munsterlander	25–29	25
Lhasa Apso	7	6–7
Lowchen	1.8–4	1.8–4
Maltese	2–4	2–4
Manchester Terrier	8	8
Mastiff	57–89	57–89

Breed	Dogs (kg)	Bitches (kg)
Miniature Pinscher	3-4	3-4
Newfoundland	64-69	50-54
Norfolk Terrier	6	6
Norwegian Buhund	15	14
Norwich Terrier	6	6
Old English Sheepdog	27-41	23-27
Pekingese	5	5.5
Papillon	1.5-2	2-3
Pharaoh Hound	23	20
Pointer	23-25	23-25
Pomeranian	1.8-2	2-2.5
Poodle (Miniature)	5.5-7	5.5-7
Poodle (Standard)	20-31	20-31
Poodle (Toy)	3.5-5.5	3.5-5.5
Pug	6.3-8.1	6.3-8.1
Pyrenean Mountain Dog	min. 50	min. 40
Retriever (Curly Coated)	32-36	32-36
Retriever (Flat Coated)	25-35	25-34
Retriever (Golden)	31.7-36.3	27.2-31.7
Retriever (Labrador)	35	30
Rhodesian Ridgeback	34-38.5	29.5-34
Rottweiler	45.5-54.5	36-41
St Bernard	73-78	63.5-73.5

Breed	Dogs (kg)	Bitches (kg)
Saluki	20–27	16–23
Samoyed	20–25	16–20.5
Schipperke	5.4–7.3	5.4–7.3
Schnauzer	16–20.5	16–20.5
Schnauzer (Giant)	41–50	41–50
Schnauzer (Miniature)	7–8	7–8
Scottish Terrier	8.5–10.5	8.5–10.5
Sealyham Terrier	9.1	8.2
Setter (English)	20.4–30	23–27.5
Setter (Gordon)	29.5	25.5
Setter (Irish)	27–30	25–27
Shetland Sheepdog	8–10	8–10
Shih Tzu	4.5–8.1	4.5–8.1
Siberian Husky	20–27	16–23
Skye Terrier	11.3	10.5
Soft Coated Wheaten	16–20.5	16–20.5
Spaniel (Clumber)	25–32	20–27
Spaniel (Cocker)	12.7–14.5	12.7–14.5
Spaniel (Cocker, American)	11–13	11–13
Spaniel (Field)	18–25	18–25
Spaniel (Irish Water)	27	27
Spaniel (Springer, Welsh)	16–20.5	16–20.5
Spaniel (Springer, English, Sussex)	23	23

Breed	Dogs (kg)	Bitches (kg)
Staffordshire Bull Terrier	13–17	11–15.5
Stumpy Tail Cattle Dog	20–22	20–22
Tibetan Terrier	11–13.5	11–13.5
Weimaraner	25–30	20–35
Welsh Corgi (Cardigan)	9.1–11.8	9–10
Welsh Corgi (Pembroke)	10–12	10–11
Welsh Terrier	9–9.5	9–9.5
West Highland White Terrier	8–9	7–8
Whippet	10–13	8–11
Yorkshire Terrier	3	3

INDEX

A

aerosol safety
   fish 96
   and hermit crabs
      139
algae
   birdbaths 84–5,
      154
   canvas, pavers and
      vinyl 154
   fish tanks 91, 93,
      95, 154
allergies
   cats 41
   guinea pigs 130
antiseptic cream safety
   61
ants 151
apartment living
   cats 41
   dogs 7
   fish 90
   pet loo 35
apple stains 210
aquariums *see* fish
      tanks
aviaries 85
avocado stains 210

B

babies and cats 65
banana stains 210
barking, preventing 10
bathing

birds 81, 83
cats 57–8
dogs 25–7
ferrets 137
horses 106
bathtub, cleaning 43
beanbag beds 34
bedding
   cats 56, 65
   dogs 23–4, 33–5
   ferrets 137
   guinea pigs 129,
      130
   horses 114
   rabbits 124–5
birds 71–88
   attracting 80
   aviaries 85
   bathing 81, 83
   cages 73, 83–5
   chickens 85–7
   choosing 73
   clipping 81–2
   deterring 75, 78
   ducks 88
   feeding 73–4
   grooming 81–3
   health care 85
   perches 93–4
bird poo
   cage wire 155
   canvas 80
   car 74, 155
   fabric 75, 155–6

glass 79, 156
outdoor furniture
   78
powder-coated
   surfaces 78–9,
   156–7
timber 77–8
upholstery 75–6,
   155–6
wrought iron 80
birdbaths
   algae in 84–5, 154
   choosing 83
birth stains
   carpets 64, 157–8
   leather shoes 63–4,
      158
   timber and pavers
      64, 158
   upholstery 157–8
black mite 26
blankets, cleaning 34,
      158–9
bleach safety 10, 46
blood stains
   carpet 29, 62,
      81–2, 159–60
   fabric 63, 160
   mattress 160–1
   upholstery 62,
      159–60
blueberry stains 210
bones 27
boots *see* footwear

bowls *see* food and water bowls
bran ball 204
brushing
    cats 54
    dogs 25
    guinea pigs 129
    rabbits 123

C
cages
    birds 73, 83–5
    cleaning 84, 155
    rats and mice 133–4
canvas
    algae 154
    bird poo 80
    flying fox poo 148–9
    saddle pads 108
caramel-coloured poo
    carpets 13, 184–5
    dogs 8, 13
    upholstery 184–5
caramel-coloured vomit
    carpets 20, 51, 184–5, 199
    cars 37, 162
    cats 51
    dogs 20, 37, 162
    mattresses 200–1
    upholstery 184–5, 199
carbohydrate stains 178, 210
carpets
    birth stains 64, 157–8

blood stains 29, 81–2, 159–60
cleaner formula 205
dander 164–5
diarrhoea, guinea pig 128
diarrhoea, rabbit 119–20
discoloured 18–19, 53
dyeing 99
flooded 99, 163, 201
fur ball stain 65
grass stains 172–3
ice cream 174–5
ointment stains 180–1
patching 53
pet hair 24, 138, 173
petroleum jelly 33, 183
poo stains 132–4, 184–5
poo stains, caramel-coloured 13, 184–5
poo stains, cat 45
poo stains, chicken 86–7
poo stains, dog 12–14
poo stains, duck 88
poo stains, ferret 135
poo stains, turtle 142–3

saliva stains 188
spot cleaner 18
steam cleaning formula 204
toothpaste 193
urine stains 195–6
urine stains, cat 47, 53
urine stains, chicken 86–7
urine stains, dog 16–17, 18
urine stains, ferret 136
urine stains, guinea pig 126–7
urine stains, rabbit 121–2
urine stains, rat or mouse 131–2
vomit 198–9
vomit, caramel-coloured 20, 51, 184–5, 199
vomit, cat 50–1
vomit, dog 20–1
vomit, turtle 141–2
carriers for guinea pigs 130
carrot stains 210
cars
    bird poo 74, 155
    caramel-coloured vomit 37
    cat urine 69
    cleaning interior 161–3
    dog smell 38
    dog vomit 36–7, 162

ferrets in 139
saliva stains 21, 187
cats 39–70
  allergies to 41
  antiseptic cream 61
  babies and 65
  bedding 56, 65
  brushing 54
  choosing 41
  collars 58–9
  curfew 66
  dander 54, 56, 164–5
  delivering a litter 63–4
  deterring 43, 61, 66, 69
  ears 58
  enclosures 66, 68
  excessive grooming 56
  exercise 142
  feeding 9, 41–2
  fleas 58, 65
  fur balls 65, 172
  grooming 54–9
  health care 54–65
  holidays 70
  litter tray 44, 176
  maximum number of 56
  moving house 56
  overweight 42
  paws 54
  protecting laundry from 43
  removing extra hair 57
  saliva stains 52, 187
  scratching posts 59
  scratching the furniture 59
  toys 68
  travelling with 69
  vomit on carpets 50–1
  washing 57–8
  water 42
  wounds 61
cat flaps 66
cat hair
  carpets 24
  matting 54
  minimising 57
  upholstery 24, 57
cat poo
  carpets 45
  diet 41
cat towers 67
cat urine 46–50
  car 69
  carpet 47, 53
  curtains 51–2
  diet 41
  mattress 49
  stone 47–8
  terracotta 50
  timber 48–9
  upholstery 52
cereal stains 210
cheese 14
chewing
  electrical cords 9
  timber furniture 19
chickens 85–7
chicken coops 87

chicken poo on carpets and upholstery 86–7
choosing a pet
  birds 73
  cats 41
  dogs 7
  fish 91
claws, clipping dog's 27
cleaning see also bathing; stains
  bathtub 43
  birdbaths 154
  blankets 34, 158–9
  bowls see food and water bowls
  cages 84, 155
  carpets see carpets
  cars see cars
  clothing see clothing
  collars 31, 58–9, 164
  copper 109
  curtains 51–2
  fabric see fabric
  feeding areas 10–11
  fish tanks 92–5, 97, 168–70
  floors see floors
  food bowls 9, 161
  furniture see furniture
  glass see glass
  hard surface cleaner formula 206

harnesses 31, 108, 164
horse tack 107–13, 186–7
hutches 129, 174
kennels 34–5, 176
leads 164
leather see leather
litter tray see litter trays
mattress see mattress
pavers see pavers
poo stains see poo
powder-coated surfaces 78–9, 149
rat and mouse cages 133
rubber 110, 113, 191
saddles and saddle pads 107–9, 186–7
satin 189
seed containers 73
shoes see footwear
snake enclosures 145
stables 105, 114
terracotta see terracotta
tiles 50, 127
timber see timber
toys 35–6, 194–5
upholstery see upholstery
wrought iron 80
cleaning product safety
cats 54

ferrets 137
hermit crabs 139
storage 55
clipping dog's claws 27
clipping wings 81–2
clothing
grass stains 110
horse manure and urine 104
leather dye marks 112–13
soil on 111–12
cockroach baits 11
collars, cleaning 31, 58–9, 164
cooling see temperature regulation
copper, cleaning 109
coprophagia 128
cork floors, cleaning 55
cotton see fabric
crabs 139–40
curfew for cats 66
curtains, cat urine on 51–2

D
dander
birds 83
cats 54, 56, 164–5
dental care, dog's 27
desexing
cats 41
dogs 7
deterrents
birds 75, 78
cats 43, 61, 66, 69
dogs 20
fleas 170–1

flying foxes 149
pests 150–2
possums 147
rabbits 123
spiders 150–1
diarrhoea see also poo
carpets 119–20, 128, 165–6
fabric 120, 166
upholstery 119–20, 128, 165–6
diet see feeding
digging, preventing 15
disease see health care
dogs 5–38
barking 10
bedding 23–4, 33–5
brushing 25
chewing electrical cords 9
chewing furniture 19
choosing 7
clipping claws 27
cockroach baits 11
collars 31, 164
dental care 27
deterring 20
diet 8
dry nose 33
ears 26
feeding 7–10
fleas 32, 34
food bowls 9–10
grooming 23–7
harnesses 31, 164
health care 23–7, 31–3
keeping cool 10
kennels 34–5, 176

off the furniture 11
overfeeding 11
removing soil from 26–7
saliva 21–3
swimming 27
tear stains 30
ticks 17, 31, 192
toys 35–6
travelling with 36–8
washing 25–7
weight 33, 214–20
dog coat oil on fabric 167–8
dog hair, removing from furniture and carpet 24
dog poo
  bagging 15
  carpet cleaning 12–14
  coloured 13–14
  diet 8
dog urine
  on carpet 16–17, 18
  cleaning 15–18
  on stone/timber 18
dog vomit
  carpet 20–1
  inside car 36–7, 162–3
drool see saliva stains
dry bath for dogs 26
ducks 88
duck poo on carpet 88
dyeing carpets 99

E
ears
  cat's 58
  dog's 26
egg stains 210
electrical cord safety 9, 124
enclosures see also cages; hutches; tanks
  cats 66, 68
  chicken coops 87
  ferrets 137
  guinea pigs 129–30
  hermit crabs 139–40
  snakes 144–5
  spiders 146
  turtles 143
enzyme-based cleaners 46
exercise for cats 42
exfoliation 26

F
fabric see also clothing; upholstery; wool
  bird poo 75, 80, 155–6
  blood stains 63, 160
  cat saliva 52
  dirt 166–7
  dog coat oil 167–8
  dog saliva 22–3
  flying fox poo 149
  grass stains 172–3
  ice cream 175
  ointment stains 181–2
  petroleum jelly 183
  rabbit diarrhoea 120
  satin 110
  silk 75
  stain removers 209–11
  toothpaste 193–4
  vomit 200
  wool 183, 193–4
fabric toys, cleaning 35, 194–5
faeces see poo
fat stains 178–9, 210–11
feather dust (dander) 83
feathers 82
feeding see also food and water bowls
  birds 73–4
  cats 9, 41–2
  chickens 86
  cleaning the area 10–11
  dogs 7–10
  ferrets 135
  fish 91
  guinea pigs 126
  horses 103
  rabbits 119
  rats and mice 131
  spiders 146
  turtles 140, 143
ferrets 134–9
  bathing 137
  bedding 137
  enclosures 137
  feeding 135
  fleas 137

food bowls 135
grooming 137
hair on carpet and
    upholstery 138
poo stains on
    carpet 135
travelling with 139
urine stains on
    carpet 136
water 135
filters for fish tanks
    95–7
fish 89–100
choosing 91
feeding 91
outdoor ponds 100
fish tanks 91–8
algae 91, 93, 95,
    154
choosing 91–2
cleaning 92–5, 97,
    168–70
filters 95–7
maintenance 97
mould 96
plants for 95
repairing 98
temperature 92,
    96, 97
fleas
cats 58, 65
deterring 170–1
dogs 32, 34
ferrets 137
guinea pigs 129
flies 11, 107, 151
flooding 9, 163, 201
floors
carpeted see
    carpets

feathers on 82
timber 55
flyblown ears 26
flying fox poo 148–9
food see feeding
food and water bowls
cats 42
cleaning 9, 161
dogs 9–10
ferrets 135
rabbits 119
food stains 210–11
footwear
birth stains 63–4,
    158
cleaning 113
horse manure
    104–5
poo stains 185–6
removing smells
    192
rubber 191
shoe frou formula
    206
fragrance (perfume) 11
freshwater fish 91
frogs 148
fruit flies 152
fruit stains 210–11
fur see hair
fur ball stain 65, 172
furniture see also
    timber;
    upholstery
cat scratching 59
dog saliva 22–3
keeping dogs off
    11
outdoor 78, 156–7
pet hair 24, 134

polish formula
    205
puppy chewing 19

G
glass
bird poo 79, 156
'cancer' 97
mould 177
saliva stains 188
glycerine solution
    formula 205
goldfish 92, 98
grass stains 110,
    172–3
grooming see also
    bathing;
    brushing
birds 81–3
cats 54–9
dogs 23–7
ferrets 137
guinea pigs 129
horses 106–7
rabbits 123
guinea pigs 126–31
allergies to 130
bedding 129, 130
carriers 130
diarrhoea 128
eating their poo
    128
enclosures and
    hutches
    129–30
feeding 126
fleas 129
grooming 129
keeping cool 130
urine stains 126–7

H

hair
  cat's *see* cat hair
  dog's 24
  rabbit's 124
  rat's 134
  on carpets 24, 173
  on fabric and
    upholstery
    134, 138, 173
  on hard surfaces
    173
hair, bird poo in 75
halters, cleaning
  110–11
hard surface cleaner
  formula 206
harnesses, cleaning 31,
  108, 164
health care *see also*
    safety
  birds 85
  cats 54–65
  dogs 23–7, 31–3
  horses 109
  rats and mice 134
heat exhaustion, dogs'
  10
hermit crabs 139–40
holidays, caring for
    your cat during
    70
horses 101–15
  bedding 114
  feeding 103
  grooming 106–7
  pests 106–7
  saliva 106
  stables 114
  sun protection 109

travelling with 115
  trough 103
  washing 106
  water 103
horse manure and
    urine
  clothing 104
  leather boots
    104–5, 113
  stable walls 105–6
  uses 114
hutches
  cleaning 174
  guinea pigs 129–30
  rabbits 124–5
hygiene *see* bathing;
    grooming;
    health care

I

ice cream 174–5
ink stains 179
iron, bird poo on 80

K

kennels, cleaning 34–5,
  176
kittens, delivering 63–4
kitty litter *see* litter trays

L

laundry, protecting
    from cats 43
lavender mix formula
  206
leads, cleaning 111–13,
  164
leather
  birth stains 63–4,
    158

conditioner
    formula 21,
    205
  dirt 167
  horse manure
    104–5, 113
  poo stains 185–6
  saddles 107–8,
    186–7
  saliva stains 22,
    188
  scratch marks 28–
    9, 60–1, 190
leather dye marks
  112–13
licences
  native animals
    146–7
  snakes 144
light requirement of
    turtles 143
litter trays
  cats 44, 176
  ferrets 137
  rabbits 121, 124

M

maggots 11
manure *see* poo
matting
  cats 54
  rabbits 123
mattress
  blood stains 160–1
  cat urine 49
  vomit 200–1
mice *see* rats and mice
microchipping
  cats 41
  dogs 7

milk stains 211
mint tea formula 206
mosquitoes 97, 150
mould
    fish tanks 96
    glass 177
    home entrance 16
    removing with
        slugs 152
    stables 114
moving house with
    cats 56

N
native animals 146–50
native birds 73
nose, dog's 33

O
oil stains 30, 178–9,
    210–11
ointment stains 180–2
outdoor furniture, bird
    poo on 78, 156–7
overfeeding dogs 11
overweight cats 42
oxide stains 180

P
paint stains 179
pavers
    algae 154
    birth stains 63, 158
paws
    cat's 54
    dog's 26
pea stains 211
pear stains 211
pebbles in fish tank,
    cleaning 96

pee *see* urine stains
perches 93–4
pests 150–2 *see also*
        deterrents
    ants 151
    black mite 26
    fleas *see* fleas
    flies 11, 107, 151
    fruit flies 152
    of horses 106–7
    mosquitoes 97,
        150
    snails and slugs
        151–2
    spiders 150–1
    ticks 17, 31, 192
pet loo 35, 182
pet rescue options 7
petroleum jelly 33, 183
pigment stains 179–80
plants
    attracting birds 80
    for fish tanks 95
    for pond 100
plastic, scratch marks
        on 190
polyurethane
    scratch marks on
        61, 190
    testing for 207
ponds 100, 148
poo 184–6 *see also*
        diarrhoea; litter
        trays
    bird's *see* bird poo
    caramel-coloured
        see caramel-
        coloured poo
    cat's 44–5

chicken's 86–7
dog's *see* dog poo
ferret's 135
flying fox 148–9
guinea pig's 128
horse's *see* horse
        manure and
        urine
rabbit's 119, 124
rats and mice
        132–3
turtle's 142–3
on carpet 184–5
on shoes 185–6
on timber walls
        186
on upholstery
        184–5
possums 147–8
pot plants 61
potty patch 35
powder-coated
        surfaces
    bird poo on 78–9
    flying fox poo 149
pregnant women
    and cats 45
    and fleas 170
protein stains 178, 211
pumpkin stains 211
puppy farms 7

Q
quolls 147

R
rabbits 119–25
    bedding 124–5
    deterring 123
    diarrhoea 119–20

feeding 119
grooming 123
litter box 121
play 125–6
poo 119, 124
urine stains 121–3
rabbit hair
making wool or
felt 124
matting 123
removing from
upholstery 124
railings, bird poo on
156–7
rainbow lorikeets 74, 80
rats and mice 131–4
cages 133–4
feeding 131
hair on couch 134
health care 134
poo stains on
carpet 132–3
teeth 133
urine stains on
carpet 131–2
resin stains 180
riding gear, cleaning
108
rosemary tea 25
rubber, cleaning 110,
113, 191
rust stains 179–80

S
saddle pads 108
saddles, cleaning
107–8, 186–7
safety see also health
care
aerosols 96, 139

antiseptic cream
61
babies and cats 65
balconies 41
bleach 10, 46
bones 27
cat litter trays 45
cleaning products
see cleaning
product safety
cockroach baits 11
dog's diet 8
electrical cords 9,
124
enzyme-based
cleaners 46
flea deterrents 170
fragrance
(perfume) 11
washing machines
and cats 54
saliva stains 187–9
cats 52, 187
dog 21–3
horse 106
on car 187
on carpets 188
on glass 188
on leather 188–9
on upholstery 188
satin 110, 189
scratch marks 190–1
leather 28–9, 60–1,
190
plastic 190
polyurethane 61,
190
stainless steel 191
timber 61, 191
vinyl 191

scratching posts 59
seagull poo on canvas
80
sealant, testing 207
seed containers,
cleaning 73
shellac, testing for 207
shoe frou formula 206
shoes see footwear
silk, bird poo on 75
sleep see bedding
slugs 151–2
snails 151–2
snakes 144–5
soil
on clothing 111–12
on dogs 26–7
spiders
deterring 150–1
as pets 145–6
spot cleaner for carpet
18
squeaky toys, cleaning
35, 194
stables 105, 114
stainless steel, scratch
marks on 191
stains see also cleaning
birthing see birth
stains
blood see blood
stains
carbohydrates 178,
210
cereal 210
dog coat oil 167–8
fat 178–9, 210–11
food 210–11
fruit 210–11
fur ball 65, 172

grass 110, 172–3
ice cream 174–5
ink 179
leather dye marks 112–13
milk 211
mould *see* mould
oil 30, 178–9, 210–11
ointment 180–2
oxide 180
paint 179
pigments 179–80
poo *see* diarrhoea; poo stains
proteins 178, 211
resin 180
rust 179–80
saliva *see* saliva stains
soil *see* soil
spot cleaner 18
sugar 178
sunscreen 211
tannin 205
tears 30
toothpaste 193–4
urine *see* urine stains
vegetable 210–11
vomit *see* vomit
watermarks 37
starchy stains 178
stone, urine stains on 18, 47–8, 196
suckerfish 97
sugar stains 178
sun protection for horses 109
sunscreen stains 211

surface sealant, testing for 207
sweet potato stains 211
swimming, dogs 27

T
tanks
    fish *see* fish tanks
    hermit crabs 139–40
    turtles 143
tannin stains 205
tartar 27
tear stains 30
teeth
    dogs 27
    rats 133
temperature regulation
    dogs 10
    fish tanks 92, 96, 97
    guinea pigs 130
    hermit crabs 139
    snakes 144
    turtles 143
tennis balls, cleaning 35–6
terracotta
    sealing 50
    urine stains 50, 198
ticks 17, 31, 192
tiles
    guinea pig urine 127
    sealing 50
timber *see also* furniture
    birth stains 64, 158

floors 55
mould 177
poo stains 186
poo stains, bird 77–8
puppy chewing 19
scratch marks 61, 191
toothpaste 193
urine stains 197
urine stains, cat 48–9
urine stains, dog 18–19
urine stains, rabbit 122–3
tomato stains 211
toothpaste stains 193–4
toxoplasmosis 45
toys
    cats 68
    cleaning 35–6, 194–5
    dogs 35–6
travelling
    with cats 69
    with dogs 36–8
    with ferrets 139
    with horses 115
tropical fish 91
troughs 103
turtles 140–3
    exposure to light 143
    feeding 140, 143
    poo stains on carpet 142–3
    tanks and enclosures 143

vomit stains
on carpet/
upholstery 141

U

upholstery
birth stains 157–8
blood stains 62,
159–60
dander 164–5
diarrhoea, guinea
pig 128
diarrhoea, rabbit
119–20
grass stains 172–3
ice cream 174–5
oily marks 30
ointment stains
180–1
pet hair 24, 57,
124, 138
petroleum jelly 183
poo stains 184–5
poo stains, bird
75–6, 155–6
poo stains,
caramel-
coloured
184–5
poo stains, chicken
86–7
saliva stains 188
toothpaste 193
urine stains 195–6
urine stains, cat 52
vomit 198–9
vomit, caramel-
coloured
184–5, 199
vomit, turtle 141–2

urine stains 195–8
cats see cat urine
dogs see dog urine
ferrets 136
guinea pigs 126–7
horses 104
rabbits 121–3
rats and mice
131–2

V

vaccinations
cats 41
dog 7
varnish, testing for 207
Vaseline stains 33, 183
vegetable stains
210–11
venomous snakes 144
vinyl
algae 154
scratch marks 191
vomit 198–201
carpets 184–5,
198–9
carpets, cat's 50–1
carpets, dog's 20–1
carpets, turtles
141–2
cars 37, 162–3
mattresses 200–1
upholstery 184–5,
199

W

walking the dog 10
walls, poo stains on
186
washing machines and
cats 54

washing your pet see
bathing
water
bowls see food
and water
bowls
cats 42
ferrets 135
flooding 99, 163,
201
hermit crabs 140
horses 103
snakes 144
temperature see
temperature
regulation
turtles 143
water fountains 42
water hyacinth 100
water lilies 100
watermark, removing
37
watermelon stains 211
wax finishes, testing
for 207
weed killer, rabbit poo
as 119
weight, dogs' 33,
214–20
wild birds 74
wings, clipping 81–2
wood see timber
wool
petroleum jelly 183
toothpaste 193–4
wrought iron, bird poo
on 80